SKIN HUNGER

SKIN HUNGER

Guide to the Language

of Touch

Mariana M. Brosnan

Cover Photo Russell Chauncey
Cover Design Judith Lye

Published by Mariana M. Brosnan at KDP Publishing
Discover other titles by Mariana M. Brosnan at
www.MarianaMBrosnan.com

~~~~

Dedicated to Lani & Isla

The two most beautiful girls in the world

May your lives be filled with love and hugs

~~~~

Introduction

In the early 1900s extremely ill children, with undiagnosed diseases, were admitted into the hospital. A triage doctor would examine a frail little one and write 'hopeless' on their admissions chart. Although the sick children were promptly given medical assistance and proper nutrition, they wasted away and all of them died.

To find solutions, Boston physician Fritz Talbot toured a Germany hospital children's ward. He saw an older lady, assumed she was a nurse, carrying around a child. Her name was Old Anna. He found out that when any child was deemed beyond any medical intervention, their care would be handed over to Anna, for on-going, loving touch and attention beyond medical care. Anna was reported to be successful to bring those in her care back to full health. Dr. Talbot brought this loving touch technique to American hospitals and was able to start saving these very, ill children. (iluv2prshim, 2007)

We humans have an innate sense that life not only be filled with practical, material things but we also desire deep connections to one another. This wonderful feeling is expressed as electricity passes from one heart to another by a simple touch. We will feel an emptiness unless we are truly known, accepted and loved. At this develops, then we feel fully alive. We can listen and discover that our emotions can be known and understood by us and that we can know and understand others.

It is time to hit mute on the depressing news, turn off your IG alerts, put down your next cup of coffee, hit pause on life for a few minutes and really feel your own heart. This all starts with the simple act of reaching out of our own bubble and breaking gently into another's parameter. Let us create space to look deeply into the face of another and see the heart of those on this earth's journey. The most important thing begins with love, being loved and loving others.

We can move beyond meeting our own personal Skin Hunger, to expand to meet the needs of our family and friends and people we interact with. We will create in all of us balanced emotions, activated spirit, healthy body and see financial gains.

I encourage you to start from where you are today and begin to acknowledge your own needs and desires for physical contact and become aware of the needs of those around you. Be a catalyst for positive change and bring more connection to the world.

Portions of this book are works of nonfiction that are my memory from my perspective. Certain names and identifying characteristics have been changed.

ATTENTION: Several people proof this book before you received it but you may be super-sensitive to typos or other obvious mistakes. And if you are the first one to tell us, then we will send you a postcard from the country I am currently in! mailto:power2flex@gmail.com

Touch has a memory.

John Keats

Mariana M. Brosnan

Table of Contents

Preface

Growing up in a bicultural and bilingual family who lived in Alaska and Costa Rica and sometimes in-between, meant adapting my preferences of hugs and social space to adapt to other preference's as well. My Costa Rican born mother and my Irish American father were both physically affectionate to their children. Frequent intense backrubs, warm hugs and gentle kisses from them expressed their feelings. My primary love language is physical touch and I am highly sensitive to this type of contact.

Life in small-town Alaska, where fierce independence and personal freedom are valued, individualism and distinction are expressed by people building their own home with trees logged from their own property into unique log cabins. Ample social space between people is normal and less physical interaction is displayed.

My best friend in Alaska would give me a warm hug upon my return from a long absence. Beyond that we did not exchange much physical affection. A cursory big hug hello and goodbye was the norm with my father's extended family. More emphasis was on the intellectual, on our ability to relate ideas and experiences. These we shared over a big bowl of ice cream that regardless of our infrequent appearances, always seemed to be waiting for us.

By contrast, upon my arrival in Costa Rica, I would be mobbed with affection and close social space. My whole family of six would stay in one room together in the house of one of my aunts for months on end. All my extended family, the mix of cousins, grandparents, aunts and uncles converse with meaning expressed through interactive touches on the hand, arm, leg and shoulder. Normally, I could not walk through a room without someone patting my head or giving me a hug. Occasionally my aunt would give me a playful kick on the behind. As I moved back and forth between my two cultures, I had to adjust my spatial distancing and displays of affection to socially conform to how, when, and where it was appropriate.

When we would return to America, I felt that I could be more natural because I enjoyed the closeness in the Latin world. I would miss the warm interactions and feelings of love that I felt matched my needs. I would recalibrate to consciously follow societal rules.

As a long-term global traveler, I have continued to observe, interview and discuss the touch needs of others. This lack of desired touch was common to those I encountered in every country and culture, which led me to begin writing this book nearly eight years ago.

The arrival of Covid has created an environment where people fear any in-person interactions and have further detached from extended family and friends to try to be in safe space. Difficulties in the relationship continuum, the increase in social media as a substitute for in the flesh relationships and the online facade of a projected perfect life have left many people feeling isolated. More than ever humans need to intentionally connect and show support for each other.

All these events have prompted me to release this guide. I believe this offering will give you tools you can quickly implement to start bringing affirmative contact back into your life. I hope you enjoy the anecdotal stories and research studies that affirm how good touch positively effects the body, soul, mind and spirit.

Mariana M. Brosnan

Section One:

What Is Skin Hunger?

Mariana M. Brosnan

Chapter 1: I Need A Hug

Henry and his wife Mel had been married for 50 years. He had always wanted more touch with her. She had brushed off his need as sexual advances. Mel had gotten rheumatoid arthritis and Henry volunteered to give her massage to help with the pain. They were both surprised at how the touch helped reduce her pain and satisfied his desire for needed affection. The effect went beyond the physical and they developed more intimacy in their emotional relationship and they became better partners. (June 21, 2016, Personal interview, in-person meeting)

Skin hunger is caused when there is a gap between the desire and need for more skin-to-skin touch than a person receives. Each person may be getting a baseline of touch, but the deficiency is based on their own perceived need. Touch is simultaneously given and received in a physical exchange of expression between people. This contact positively reinforces each person's identity, giving the foundation for them to grow into a fuller human.

Humans have a God-given innate, natural desire to be nurtured by a loving touch. This hard-wired biology impacts the view an individual has of themselves. This basic need extends from the pre-birth state until death, for the entire life span.

Affirming skin-to-skin touch is the soothing experience of massage, hugs, hair being stroked, face being caressed, holding hands, kissing, and embrace.

The human body is an amazing creation. In one square inch of skin, there is 234 feet of nerves, 19,500 sensory cells, (end of nerve fibers), 1,300 nerve endings to record pain, 78 yards of nerves and 13 cold and 78 heat receptors. In an average adult, skin measures 21 square feet (2 meters squared). The millions of skin receptors continuously receive and transmit electronic data to be collected and categorized. Each touch is discerned as either pleasant, enjoyable, and desired to be repeated or as rough, undesired, and to be avoided. These receptors analyze the touch and interpret, based on the type of touch, if their identity is affirmed or rejected. (Montagu, 1971) The body captures the experiences that can bring satisfaction and connect the soul. The mind teaches the skin to avoid people who disrespect the person.

The effects of people feeling disconnected from others is a too-common theme around the world. I have traveled the world for eight years and have been recording conversations with travelers. Most people reported that they might accidentally touch another human, but in their day to day, their touch needs were not satisfied. Here are some examples from different ages and backgrounds.

Swedish, age 29, woman who said she had made dental appointments to get some physical touch when she was not in a dating relationship (March 4, 2019, Personal interview, in-person meeting)

Japanese, age 21, man said, "no one touches each other in Japan." (May 7, 2013, Personal interview, in-person meeting)

Russian, age 25, woman found it difficult to find friends to have affection and not have it be awkward (April 3, 2018, Personal interview, in-person meeting)

American, age 70, he had a nanny as a child and he felt it was the only time he had enough affirming touch in his whole life (May 15, 2014, Personal interview, in-person meeting)

Despite these people working hard to be in relationships or in friendships they did not feel satisfied with the affection received. The feedback of touch-deprivation was remarkably similar regardless of the country, gender, age, religion or culture. Each person innately felt that the lack of touch was negatively impacting their life. This lack of touch causing harm to health was accidently discovered during the middle ages in a language experiment.

The Roman emperor Fredrick II conducted an experiment to see what language a baby would speak if she were not exposed to any language. Fredrick had fifty infants removed from their parents at birth. The child's physical needs of food, clean diapers, warmth and shelter were provided. The nurses were instructed to not cuddle or speak to the children. Despite having their basic needs of food and shelter met, all the infants died. The children could not survive the absence of human touch and their deaths were attributed to 'failure to thrive'. (Breen and

Profile, 2020) This medical situation occurs in infants where their physical or mental development fails to progress due to missing skin-to-skin contact or other medical or underlying problem. (Stawar, 2018)

Starting with the very young, across all ages there has been an increase in loneliness in the last century. Cigna, a health insurance and wellness company, studied how loneliness, health and job satisfaction correlate. Their January 2020 report shows that loneliness is up to 61 percent, an increase of six percent over the last two years. Over half of Boomers (56-74) at 53 percent feel lonely. The disconnect socially is hitting hardest the Gen Zers, (18-22) with nearly 3 in 4 feeling lonely some or all the time. (Cigna, 2020) The loss of social communities to find connection and our place in society has left people feeling isolated, unsure and unwell.

In 2018, the U.K. Appointed a Loneliness Minister, Tracey Crouch in response to a report that 14 percent or nine million people feel lonely at least often. People who do not have a well-established social or work network such as recent immigrants, the disabled or unemployed are experiencing the worst without relief. (John, 2018)

These are two examples in the Western world of a lack of connection to others. Without having the necessary skin-to-skin contact that each person needs, people will wither emotionally and physically.

Feed Your Skin Activities

Have a 20-second hug with each of your

family members or roommates in your home

today. Give a coworker a pat on the shoulder.

Pet your cat or dog for five minutes. Give

yourself a neck massage to ease the stress.

* * * *

Brindley, E., 2020. The Hartford Courant – Coronavirus Medical Workers Precautions. [online] Courant.com. Available at: <https://www.courant.com/coronavirus/hc-news-coronavirus-medical-workers-precautions-20200323-d267wtsbqfdpxgt5xd3q5n4uam-story.html> [Accessed 30 May 2020].

Breen, B. and Profile, V., 2020. A Medieval Emperor's Natural Language Experiment. [online] Resobscura.blogspot.com. Available at: <https://resobscura.blogspot.com/2018/05/a-medieval-emperors-natural-language.html> [Accessed 16 November 2018].

Cigna.com. 2020.Cigna 2020 Loneliness Report. [online] Available at: <https://www.cigna.com/static/www-cigna-com/docs/about-us/newsroom/studies-and-reports/combatting-loneliness/cigna-2020-loneliness-report.pdf> [Accessed 4 May 2020].

iluv2prshim. (2007, January 9). Children are to be Loved. Iluv2prshim. https://iluv2prshim.wordpress.com/2007/02/09/children-are-to-be-loved/

John, T. (2018, April 25). Tracey Crouch UK Loneliness Minister. Time. https://time.com/5248016/tracey-crouch-uk-loneliness-minister/

Lee, C., Cadigan, J., & Rhew, I. (2020, October 21). Increases in Loneliness Among Young Adults During the COVID-19 Pandemic and Association With Increases in Mental Health Problems. PubMed Central (PMC). https://www.ncbi.nlm.nih.gov/pmc/articles/PMC7576375/

Menon, P., 2020. Out Of Touch? | Chennai News - Times Of India. [online] The Times of India. Available at: <https://timesofindia.indiatimes.com/city/chennai/out-of-touch/articleshow/76915560.cms> [Accessed 16 July 2020].

Milan, A., 2020. Coronavirus: How Long Was Wuhan In Lockdown And What Are The New Rules? | Metro News. [online] Metro.co.uk. Available at: <https://metro.co.uk/2020/04/09/long-wuhan-lockdown-rules-china-12534667/> [Accessed 15 July 2020].

Montagu, A. (1971). Touching: The Human Significance of the Skin (First Edition). Columbia Univ Pr.

Stawar, T. (2018, January 25). The importance of touch. News and tribune. http://www.newsandtribune.com/opinion/stawar-the-importance-of-touch/article_9f923450-0159-11e8-805d-836329c9528c.html

Ufberg, M., 2020.I'M Stuck In A Hotel Room In India. I Don'T Know When I'Ll Get Home.. [online] Medium. Available at: <https://gen.medium.com/im-stuck-in-a-hotel-room-in-india-i-don-t-know-when-i-ll-get-home-22f758b03657> [Accessed 17/7/2020].

~~~~

Chapter 2: What Is Blocking Us From Getting Touch?

There were 10 of us meeting for drinks. As soon as we all arrived, we would stack all the cell phones in the center of the table. We would order drinks and talk and laugh. Occasionally someone would reach for their phone and we would all pause and look to see if they would touch it. The game was that the first one to check their phone paid for all the drinks.

Technology was designed and marketed for connection and to lessen loneliness feelings. From the telegraph machine to telephone to social media and cell phones, new inventions promised to help us "reach out and touch someone," as in the famous quote from Ma Bell. While having access to being virtually connected nearly-continuously, technology has squashed the need for in-person human exchange. People touch their smartphones on average 2,617 times a day. (Nelson, 2016) Some of the usage is legit to access information and some is FOMO-fear of missing out of activities- or keep track of online posts. We spend time electronically trying to impress people who we may never meet. Couples, going out to dinner, spend more time looking at their phone than interacting with each other. (Fernandez & Matt, 2019)

A Touch Research Institute study in airports around the world show people interacting with their phones only for 98 percent of the time. (Jones, 2018) It has become common to justify that cell phones are necessary but 1 in 4 couples has said that their partner is spending too much on screen time. One in ten couples have had an argument regarding the time or content on the phone with their partner. People use their phones at their child's sports event, in their car, during mealtimes with family, in the bathroom and take their phones to bed, being available 24 hours a day. (Good Therapy Staff, 2016) This psychological thrill that our brains receive when we get a message or a "like" on a post keeps us pursuing an intangible online connection as we miss the possibility of a real life physical and emotional payoff.

Not only has technology interfered with human connection but cultural rules govern public displays of affection. This overlap of culture and touch was observed in a 1966 study, when pioneering psychologist Sidney Jourad observed conversations between friends in the United Kingdom, in France, United States and in Puerto Rico. He counted how many times the pairs touched each other during a one-hour conversation. The friends in the U.K. did not touch each other at all. The U.S. pair only made contact twice. In Paris, they touched each other while talking 110 times, which is roughly two times per minute. The Latinos in Puerto Rico had three occurrences of touch per minute. (Keltner, 2010) These different cultures had a different thought towards the usage of touch in imparting ideas.

Words and touch were used differently depending on whether there was subtext in the exchange. Communication in a low-context culture happens through exact word choices to convey ideas and essential feelings. When near emotionless thoughts or feelings are stated factually there is not much subtext. Low-context cultures like the people from United Kingdom, the United States, Austria, Canada, Germany and Scandinavian countries, will stand close enough to converse but not close enough to accidentally touch. In North America, the distance is 18" for casual conversation and in Western Europe with its high population density in urban areas the norm drops to 14-16". (Erickson, 2020) People from countries that have cooler weather tend to stand further apart than countries with warmer climates.

24

Mediterranean, Latin American, African and Middle Eastern cultures spatial norms are more intimate. France and Italy have warm, friendly, close contact in their discussions. Latin countries have high-context exchanges with touch to amplify meaning and vocal inflections. In Nigeria boisterous conversations are normal along with touching each other on the arm and shoulder. In South Africa affection displays a sense of trust to others. (Evanson, 2015) Middle Easterners traditionally have a close 8" to 12" space apart to enable smelling the other's clothing, body odors, and breath. (Hall, 1990).

Asian countries show respect by having low contact to males, older people, strangers, co-workers, or people with higher positions of authority or status. In Japan, South Korea, Taiwan and the Philippines deference is shown by giving ample physical space, bowing the head low and not touching the honored one. Public displays of affection between couples or friends are seen as disrespectful. In Thailand, people do not touch other's heads, including children. (Early & Ang, 2003) Thai consider the head as sacred, respected, and highest place both physically and spiritually on the body. (Green Thailand, 2020) Multicultural blogger Mabel Kwong, a Chinese national who grew up in Australia, Singapore and Malaysia, states that Asians tend by nature to be shy, to respect personal and physical space, and to not touch to avoid catching germs and getting dirty. (Kwong, 2020)

In each culture, social rules guide how people of different ages can engage. Young children are not restricted and enjoy the most freedom. A child can climb into their mother's lap for affection, give a bear hug around their sister's neck, wrap their arms around a father's leg, and be held by their grandma just because they want to be held. An older person may be more inhibited, have less mobility or may not have family or friends that they can get a friendly hug from. Sometimes a little one will reach out to a withdrawn older person and can really change their lives.

A recent widower, Dan, age 82, was shopping for groceries. "Hi, old person. It's my birthday today," a little four-year-old Nora said. She and her mom were shopping. Nora kept talking to Dan, she gave him a hug and wanted her picture taken with him. Dan later confessed that he had not been hugged for months until Nora had embraced him. His wife had died six months earlier and since then he had suffered from depression, had felt anxiety and had not slept well. He lived far away so he could not get affection from his own family.

Nora's mom has taken Nora to visit Dan and they have developed a friendship. Nora and Dan have a grandpa to granddaughter affectionate relationship and spend time together, celebrating birthdays and giving hugs. Dan feels like Nora literally saved his life. (Rosenblatt, 2016)

Research shows people need eight skin-to-skin touches daily for their brain to function normally, for emotions to regulate and for their body to be unstressed and resilient against disease. When I would discuss this with people I met on my travels, many asked-What is touch? I would reach over and lightly touch their arm with my fingers. Sometimes they would tap my arm while counting to eight. A few people responded to the topic of touch by immediately touching their own head, arms and legs. I would smile and respond by explaining that to be beneficial, the touch must be with another human.

Because of my openness to the discussion of touch, people quickly realized I was open to hugs and touch, they would initiate more touch with me. Sometimes they would ask me for a hug or just sit close enough our legs would brush. Both men and women seem relieved that it was not just them who craved touch and were relaxed to find a way to have safe touch.

Touch is governed by the societal rules and hierarchical rules on the job as people move into adulthood and into the workforce. Single people struggle with getting enough good physical touch. With everyone leading busy lives, it is difficult to find time and a real emotional connection. There may not be enough time when playing sports, going to church to allow space to create deep relationships. Some workplaces have regulations against dating coworkers. Without somebody to hug, a substitute is used. A stuffed animal may become someone to cuddle or pillows on both sides of the body may simulate someone else in the bed. Although these may help, it is important for single people to have close friends to get their touch needs met.

In some places around the world, the word 'touch' has been degraded to only imply a sexual experience. A young Australian woman said that she enjoys hugging people. She used to be more touchy-feely with others until both males and females misinterpreted her friendliness as a sexual advance. In America touch has been infantilized or deemed suspect as a query for sexual contact. Innocent touching has been recategorized as possible grooming, making people fearful to hug or touch someone's shoulder.

Teen boys and young males have felt that they must give up the childish affection from parents and look for a relationship to get their physical affirming needs met. Traditionally any touch from a male has been sexualized more than from a female. Many people I interviewed said they wanted to be freer with affection like a kiss on the cheek, or a hug or to cuddle up under the blankets with someone but it was difficult because their friends would misinterpret their intention.

When couples marry, they tend to have an expectation that their spouse or perhaps future children will meet their needs for physical affection. Spouses may start with a deep physical and emotional connection but find schedules, interpersonal conflict, work and children taking up time and energy and crowd out desired touch. It becomes essential to be proactive with a spouse to incorporate touch into daily relationship. It is also important to give and receive hugs outside the marriage. One way it to have a friend group to socialize and with whom you exchange warm affection.

For those in happy marriages touch can be easily implemented. Those unhappily or apathetically married may have a low desire to express any affection to their partner. When a relationship ends due to a breakup, a mental or physical illness or the loss of a spouse from divorce or death the emotional fallout of being newly single may be depressing and overwhelming. Often people may get involved physically to make up for the sudden loss of a romantic partner. It is important to allow time and space to emotionally processed the loss.

Some Western countries cultural rules are to refrain from close contacts with anyone not in the inner circle. Many people told me that they try to avoid customary social greetings with acquaintances and reserve these touches for their intimate friendships. Italians in general are known to be affectionate but one Italian guy said he did not enjoy touch with friends even as a child. When he is in a relationship where he feels permission to display his feelings, he said that he becomes very affectionate. (Personal in-person interview, July 18, 2016). Touch-feast to touch-fast was described by people who when in a romantic relationship they enjoyed a lot of good touch but when the relationship ended it dropped to zero touch.

Extroverts and introverts handle touch differently. An extrovert may give and receive an equal enthusiastic layer of attention and affection to many people. The touch is like layering of icing on a cake and any unfavorable contact can be discarded as there is a lot to choose from. On the other hand, too much social touch and too much time with other people can drain an introvert. They will be more critical of who and how possible contact can happen, often developing strategies to determine preferred touch. Because of their selectiveness, an introvert can internalize the meaning of the touch in a much deeper way than their extroverted counterparts. Both extroverts and introverts act in a way to get their baseline touch needs met.

Increasingly as people get busy, time feels compacted and insufficient to meet their own or other's needs. Starting with a new baby, parents may be exhausted due to late-night feedings, increased stress over finances or being tired at work and may not have the quantity or quality of time to soothe their newborn. American families where both mother and father work will start their 6-week-old baby in daycare. Daycare centers have a recommended ratio of one caregiver for three infants. Workers may not have time to cuddle each child sufficiently or meet their emotional needs. One child crying can be the catalyst to make others cry in sympathy causing stress for the providers. A more sensitive, caring toddler may offer a hug, taking the role of comforting a distressed friend.

Younger children may sense their parent's busyness and avoid requesting the comfort and affection that they need and try to self-soothe. Some children will find the way of least resistance by sneaking in their parent's beds at night to get desired cuddle time.

As youth bodies and minds develop, they gravitate away from their closeness with their parents and engage with their peers through social networks and media. These become the new ideals of friendliness, affection, getting attention and someone to care for you. The feelings of parents to their teens developing body and growing independence can subliminally push youth away from previous beneficial interactions of long hugs, kisses or sitting on dad's lap. A peer's disapproval of childish behaviors like kissing or hugging parents can leave a teen in a desert of untouched isolation. Emerging hormones change teens interests to attraction, romantic feelings and a desire to express the surging emotions physically. Oftentimes the cultural message is to find a romantic partner for physical contact or be isolated.

Not only in home but in the public arena as well, there is a decline in positive affirmation through healthy touch. As sexual abuse has happened in schools between adults and children or young people, School districts are establishing rules to prevent touching at school. In Toronto, Canada, teachers are told that there is "no safe touch", between adults and students. In some U.S. schools with a no-touch-policy, band teachers find it nearly impossible to teach without being able to guide the student by adjusting their fingers on the instruments.

A Western Australia school system has recently enacted a detailed document regarding appropriate conduct between teachers and students. Some restrictions include that one-on-one meetings must occur in a visible place and that: "teachers are not, in any circumstances, to engage in any act or conduct directed towards a student of a romantic or sexual nature including, but not limited to, the following: kissing and/or caressing; obscene language or gestures of a sexual nature; suggestive remarks or actions; jokes or humor of a sexual nature; unwarranted and inappropriate touching; indecent exposure; inappropriate verbal compliments by a teacher to a student; communicating or corresponding with students about sexual or personal feelings for the student; and exposure of students to the sexual behavior of others, other than in authorized curriculum resources in the context of education about healthy sexual relationships ." (Government of Western Australia, 2017) These rules endeavor to establish acceptable behavior so that touch is neutral, without sexual intent but also unfortunately prevent safe, caring touch. Some students who are in bleak or stressful home situations miss out on leaning on a caring shoulder and supportive hug.

Skin Hunger: Guide to the Language of Touch

There are times that illness can prevent human interaction, such as the worldwide pandemic that started in late 2019, Covid-19. This virus was traced to originate in Wuhan, China. (Milan, 2020) The city underwent a severe lockdown for 77 days. Chinese officials reported the outbreak to the rest of the world in December 2019. As the virus spread and most countries responded by shutting down borders and placing restrictions to stop the spread of the infection. Attempts to halt the spread prompted nations to restrict people's interactions with social distancing that further splintered community, business, extended family and friends.

People already struggled with social isolation, depression, long-term unemployment, the elderly and those living alone were stripped of any possibility of physical contact. Soon our planet of 7.8 Billion people plunged into crisis management in response to the fear of physical touch to prevent contact with a rampant deadly infection.

On March 1, 2020 Shibu Joseph flew to attend a business meeting in Doha. At the end of the meeting, he shook hands with a colleague and went to his hotel as usual. Qatar went into lockdown hours later and he has not touched another human since. He has continued working online and staying in touch with his family. He has food and a nice hotel room, but the four months of isolation and lack of touch are causing him to be stressed and anxious. (Menon, 2020)

Social distancing has caused further separations across the world. An American has been stranded in his hotel in India, where he has had no physical contact with anyone since March 1st. (Ufberg, 2020) Grandparents wave at grandchildren from the other side of a window. Children are not in school, removed from their friends and now parents are thrust into the role of substitute teacher. Adults have lost the ability to socialize in public places as bars, restaurants and social clubs are closed. Sports seasons have been cancelled.

Most business meetings and church services have adapted to Zoom meetings online. University students have moved off-campus to their home residence and completed studies alone with online classes. Hospital and care home staff, physicians and emergency workers have moved out of their homes, creating a barrier to avoid exposing their spouse and family to the illness. (Brindley, 2020) (Centers for Disease Control and Prevention. 2020) Grocery store clerks and essential workers were suspect as possible carriers of the deadly illness.

Because of Covid-19 single people are more isolated. Wilson is hugging his pillow for comfort. He lost his job due to the virus and is stuck in his house but misses the affection with others. Bjorn reflects on the last time he touched another person and looks forward to the day when he can once again shake someone else's hand. Australia's hotline Friends for Good has seen a 200 percent uptick in the last several months as people deal with imposed loneliness. (Stark, 2020) These are some of the coping mechanisms in response to the stressful time we are in.

We are grieving for the life we have lost says David Kessler. He is the world's foremost expert on grief. (Berinato, 2020) As we rang in 2020, we had a feeling that this would be the year when many things we had been waiting for would happen. Globally, 2020 has been a stressful year, from wildfires in California and Australia, floods in Indonesia, Coronavirus spread globally, locust in Africa, the killing of George Floyd and the subsequent civil unrest and earthquakes in Turkey. There was a belief to hunker-down and get through the pandemic and get back to a new normal, but the virus has not relented. Kessler identifies another type of grief as anticipatory because there is no foreseeable future of the end of the pandemic when we can feel safe again. He advises to acknowledge and work through the stages of grief and come to an acceptance.

The distancing we are currently observing has exacerbated the disconnected world we were already living in. The stress of possibly falling ill, working from home, regulations on wearing face masks, restrictions on movements, loss of jobs, inability to meet with anyone living outside our own homes, the cancellation of sports and knowing that no return to normal will happen soon, cause stress hormones to surge and suppress the immune system.

With schools closing, sports shut down and play dates cancelled, school-age children are left without their usual interactions, of wrestling, playing on the playground and throwing their arm around their best friends. Children feel confused about what is happening and struggle to stay on track educationally. Parents are in the position of substitute teacher and adjusting their jobs at home to care for their children.

To lower their risk of exposure to Covid-19, rest homes have the residents stay in their rooms and bring them their food and medications. One care home has organized playing Bingo through the intercom to keep them entertained. The elderly and people with disabilities in care facilities are restricted from contact with their relatives.

Robert Barber, 85 years old comes every day to visit his wife Lauren, who has Alzheimer's and lives in a facility. The care home is not receiving any visitors to protect the residence. He comes to his wife's window and talks to her even though she cannot understand why he cannot come in. His actions represent love and trying to overcome the separation and resonated with over four million views of the video. (Nahl, 2020)

The Touch Research Institute (TRI), in Florida is a center established with a grant from Johnson & Johnson to conduct research studies on touch in relation to health and science. Director Tiffany Field, Ph.D., focuses on infant massage and postpartum depression and pain management with massage. A research study during lockdown has surveyed how people are emotionally handling Covid-19. Sleep problems were noted by 97 percent. In their survey of 100 people 60 percent felt symptoms of skin hunger including PTSD and depression. (Kale, 2020)

We need good touch and we are being blocked by our busyness and technology has left us wanting more connectivity. Working families are tired and worn out with their children in daycare and foregoing cuddles. With the loss of normal touch, we feel isolated, alone, depressed and restricted. Covid-19 has exaggerated and amplified this blossoming problem of the lack of human contact and heightened realization of skin hunger. All these things are blocking us from getting our basic skin hunger needs met. But there's good news ahead. There are many activities and ways to connect during our lives and in these stressful disconnected times. For now, take a deep breath and enjoy the activity.

Feel Good Now Activity

Turn off your phones and leave them in another room. Sit holding a hand or touching the arm of your family member. Enjoy a conversation and focus on absorbing the nice touch. If you live alone, wrap yourself in a warm cuddly blanket. Get some oil and give yourself a hand massage.

* * * *

Berinato, S., 2020. That Discomfort You're Feeling Is Grief. [online] Harvard Business Review. Available at: <https://hbr.org/2020/03/that-discomfort-youre-feeling-is-grief> [Accessed 28 July 2020].

Centers for Disease Control and Prevention. 2020. Coronavirus Disease 2019 (COVID-19). [online] Available at: <https://www.cdc.gov/coronavirus/2019-ncov/hcp/guidance-for-ems.html> [Accessed 24 July 2020].

Early, P., & Ang, S. (2003). Cultural Intelligence: Individual Interactions Across Cultures. Stanford Business Book.

Erickson, A., 2020. What 'Personal Space' Looks Like Around The World. [online] Washington post. Available at: <https://www.washingtonpost.com/news/worldviews/wp/2017/04/24/how-close-is-too-close-depends-on-where-you-live/> [Accessed 3 September 2017].

Evanson, N., 2015. South African Culture - Communication. [online] Cultural Atlas. Available at: <https://culturalatlas.sbs.com.au/south-african-culture/south-african-culture-communication> [Accessed 3 August 2020].

Fernandez, L., & Matt, S. (2019, June 19). Bored Lonely Angry Stupid Excerpt Technology Loneliness History. Slate https://slate.com/technology/2019/06/bored-lonely-angry-stupid-excerpt-technology-loneliness-history.html

Good Therapy Staff. (2016, September 19). 3 Ways Technology Can Negatively Impact Your Relationships. Goodtherapy https://www.goodtherapy.org/blog/3-ways-technology-can-negatively-impact-your-relationships-0919167

Government of Western Australia. (2017). Teacher-Student Professional Boundaries. Government of Western Australia https://www.trb.wa.gov.au/DesktopModules/mvc/TrbDownload/PublishedDoc.aspx?number=D19/065558

Green Thailand. 2020. 7 Dos And Dont's Of Thai Cultural Etiquette. [online] Available at: <http://www.responsiblethailand.co.uk/green-tourism/7-dos-and-don-ts-of-thai-cultural-etiquette/> [Accessed 11 February 2019].

Hall, E. T. (1990). The Hidden Dimension (Anchor Books a Doubleday Anchor Book) (First Paperback Edition). Anchor. (personal space bubble

Kale, S. (2020, April 12). Skin Hunger Coronavirus Human Touch. Wired https://www.wired.co.uk/article/skin-hunger-coronavirus-human-touch

Keltner, D. (2010, September 29). Hands on Research. Greater Good. https://greatergood.berkeley.edu/article/item/hands_on_research

Kwong, M., 2020. Asian, Quiet And Introverted? It's Just The Way I Am. [online] Mabel Kwong. Available at: <https://mabelkwong.com/2017/09/21/asian-quiet-and-introverted-its-just-the-way-i-am/> [Accessed 20 April 2018].

Nahl, L. (2020, March 27). Video of man visiting his wife with alzheimers during coronavirus outbreak goes viral. CBS.12. https://cbs12.com/news/local/video-of-man-visiting-his-wife-with-alzheimers-during-coronavirus-outbreak-goes-viral

Nelson, P. (2016, July 7). We touch our phones 2617 times a day says study. Networkworld. https://www.networkworld.com/article/3092446/smartphones/we-touch-our-phones-2617-times-a-day-says-study.html

Rosenblatt, K. (2016, October 29). Georgia girl, four, forms heart-warming friendship with lonely widower, 82, after noticing him by himself in a grocery store. Dailymail. https://www.dailymail.co.uk/news/article-3884058/Georgia-girl-four-forms-heart-warming-friendship-lonely-widower-82-noticing-grocery-store.html

Stark, J., 2020. Coronavirus Shutdown Talk Is Puzzling For Australians Who Live Alone. [online] The New Daily. Available at: <https://thenewdaily.com.au/.../2020/04/07/coronavirus-scott-morrison-puzzle-single-life> [Accessed 15 April 2020].

~~~~

Mariana M. Brosnan

Chapter 3: Symptoms of Lack of Positive Touch

Do you have skin hunger quiz?

1. Do you feel lonely?
2. Are you feeling more aggressive?
3. Are you stressed about your finances?
4. Has it been more than a few days since you had meaningful touch?
5. Are you having difficulty sleeping?
6. Are you afraid of developing closer friendship for fear of losing someone?
7. Are you having sexual dysfunction?
8. Are you worried more about the future than normal?
9. Do you feel dissatisfied or anxious?
10. Is your dog or cat tired of the extra attention?
11. Do you feel a general sense of feeling unhealthy?
12. Do you feel unloved or uncared for?
13. Are you trying to self-soothe often with long baths or showers or comfy clothing?
14. Are you avoiding contact with people in your bubble for fear of illness?

If you answered yes, some or all of the time, to these questions, you may be feeling the effects of Skin Hunger.

My belief is that people need three things to have a meaningful life: acceptance, love, and life purpose. Having touch is a way that people express to one another these concepts. I believe that humans are created in the image of a relational, loving, intelligent God. The Godhead has three persons in a relationship and God offers to humans his acceptance, love and purpose for their life. The family was designed to reflect relationship and be a safe place for children to learn and grow.

Parents are the model to express acceptance, love and give purpose to their young. Wikipedia defines acceptance as "a person's assent to the reality of a situation, recognizing a process or a condition, often a negative or uncomfortable situation, without attempting to change it, protest or exit." (Acceptance, n.d.) Simply rephrased, acceptance is seeing someone, with all their strengths and weaknesses, and embracing the whole of them without rejecting or ignoring perceived negative aspects. Accepting them is not displaying external "tolerance", admiring the lovely, sweet-smelling attribute, while suppressing internal "repulsion," pretending the less appealing or offensive parts of them do not exist.

To accept another is NOT mental or verbal assent to things which are offensive, loathsome, illegal, or immoral or unethical behavior. There is not a whole-hearted agreement with everything they think or do or desire. Acceptance means that the whole of who this person is can be embraced. Acceptance alongside love can help unlock a person's potential to develop.

Love, according to Webster's definition, is "unselfish, loyal, and benevolent concern for the good of another, brotherly concern." (Merriam-Webster, 2007) Love requires looking at the needs and best interests of another over one's own. In the Bible, love is patient, kind, forgiving, and unselfish. When a choice is made from love, there has been consideration for the needs and how this decision will affect other people.

Webster's also defines Purpose as, " the aim or intention of something; the aim or goal of a person: what a person is trying to do, become." (Merriam-Webster, 2007) Purpose is finding that niche in the world where you feel deeply fulfilled by giving who you uniquely are and knowing it will enrich the world. Life purpose fulfills the individual and brings pleasure, peace, and meaning. The Scottish Olympic Gold medalist in the 400-Metre, Eric Liddell, said, "When I run, I feel God's pleasure." (Goodreads. (n.d.)

In a family with mature parents, children can feel acceptance, love and start to develop a purpose that melds with their talents and interests. Communicating these values is in part through verbal affirmation which is 30 percent of the message. Touch and body language comprise the other 70 percent of this valuable affirmation to others.

Effects on the Person

Dr. Thomas R. Verny is a prenatal and perinatal psychologist. He has demonstrated the effects of their father and mother on a person starting before conception. The parent's diet, mental and physical health, any stress will affect the baby and may extend to their grandchildren. The developing infant in the womb is extremely sensitive and internalizes the messages of his parent's feelings and attitudes toward him. His physical, emotional well-being, spiritual and financial future are shaped by the treatment he receives from the people in his close environment. (Verny & Weintraub, 2003).

Physical Effects

The mother's attitude and touch towards her child affect his development. If the mother is under stress, or in an undesired pregnancy, the child receives messages from his mother biochemically and by her lack of touch with her abdomen. He internalized the message as a rejection of himself and tries to emotionally separate himself from her to attempt to preserve himself. (Divecha, 2018)

When a child is born before full-term, he is more susceptible to the messages of rejection. A neglected, premature infant who does not receive positive touch will have slow lung development and a delay in regulation of heart rate, blood pressure and body temperature. An unprepared mother can deeply affect her child.

An infant will signal her needs to her parents by crying. When she receives an inconsistent response, they sometimes respond and other times do not, she will feel insecure about her safety in the world. She will withdraw, becoming hesitant about her environment. Her brain development delays, stress hormones flood into her body and she reverts to survival mode.

Apparently, the experiment that King Fredrick did was forgotten and a similar was repeated in a 1940 experiment. Forty infants were taken from their parents at birth. All were given warm beds, food and diaper changes. Only 20 of the babies were held. Of the group that was not cuddled, half of them died. These untouched babies had tried to get their caregivers attention to no avail. The child would lay quiet and still, staring off and then gave up living and died. Humans need touch connection for survival alongside their basic needs being met. (Joubert, 2013)

Even a short time of being ignored can cause an infant who is normally well-cared for to emotionally disengage and break down. Dr. Edward Tronick, a child development researcher from Harvard University, conducted a still-face experiment. The experiment had three phases. First the parent interacted as they normally would with their infant, who was sitting in a highchair or stroller. There were certain rehearsed cues between the pair to engage each other. When the parent was cued, she would turn her face away and then turn back towards her child with a still face. No matter what cues or attempts at play and interaction her child gave her, the mother did not respond. The child who is dependent on their responsive parent would go through their play routine. He would keep trying to interact, initiating all the old familiar games, and when he did not get any response, he would escalate his attempts by crying or he would begin to hit himself. Some infants would squirm or discontinue from trying to get their parent to reengage. On the next cue the mother would turn her head away and then turn back and reengaged in their normal play interaction. The child would joyfully respond.

Even though it was for a brief time for infants who were used to normal care, they would quickly fall into despair, lose interest and become emotionally unbalanced. For example, one boy knew the familiar game between himself and his mother and felt confused when she failed to engage as normal. He would be unable to contain his disappointment and the negative feelings he was having from being ignored. He would resort to withdrawing to avoid feeling the unpleasant experience. (Gregory, 2020)

The response of lack of touch on the body are to increase anxiety levels, depression, hyperactivity, inattention, stress hormones and cortisol levels. Cortisol suppresses the immune system, making it difficult for the body to fight off disease. Without enough positive contact, inflammatory cytokines increase, which are linked to autoimmune diseases.

Field's research studies have shown lack of touch boosts digestive disorders, the symptoms of fibromyalgia, frequent headaches, insomnia from stress, myofascial pain syndromes (pain is referred from one part of the body to another), an increase in paresthesia (feeling of burning or pins and needles, skin crawling, itching or numbness), and magnifies nerve pain. Soft tissue strains and sports injuries and TMJ are more frequent. Pain is felt more sharply when no one offers comforting touch. There is an increase in intestinal distress and irregularity. Many physical consequences happen because of insufficient positive interaction. (Chillot, 2013)

Mental/well-being

Overuse of technology is disturbing mental health in families. Brandon McDaniel, an assistant professor in Human Development and Family Studies sees that parents are more distracted and not training their children. He coined the term "technoference" as the parent becomes more involved in their phone, the child's behavior keeps getting worse to draw their parents' attention. The parent may look up from the phone to quiet the child but return to the phone. The child then does something more outrageous to get the parent off the phone. (Halton, 2020)

More people are working from home and using technology to stay connected to family and friends. Phones are a distraction as people pick up and look at their phone 150 times a day.

(Fernandez, Matt, 2019) Parents are starring at their electronic devices and ignoring their babies and the effect is the same as the still-face experiment. When an infant goes to signal her father for interaction, his attention to his phone stops the reciprocal exchange and they miss a chance for the child to learn.

A study across forty-nine societies examined the correlation between affection and actions. Neuropsychologist Prescott concluded that violent behavior in adults was due to a lack of pleasurable touch in their early years. (James, 1975) Children who are not nurtured by their mothers have smaller memory and learning capacities. Neglected children can have feelings of inadequacy, and experience great difficulty to set and achieve goals in their life. The children have learned not to trust any promises and cannot show patience for delayed gratification. As adults they tend to be high conflict, show poor cooperation and have authority related problems. The results are these low-touched children face greater isolation, higher suicide rates and higher risk of a premature death.

Without touch, people can develop warped views of physical interaction. She may view touch as an invitation only for sexual contact. She may not differentiate affirmative touch from people in authority but may be unable to process this as intended. She may respond in a strong negative way or try to detach from those who are being friendly and offering contact.

A German study found that even as adults, this lack of affection affects mood and performance in life. Men who do not kiss their wife as they leave for work in the morning have a 50 percent increase in having a car accident. The depressed feeling impacts his ability to focus and drive safely. (Bloom & Bloom, 2019)

Spiritual

The spirit of a lonely human feels rejected and unloved. The lack of nourishment to their body can make them feel depressed and hopeless. In Jeremiah 17:9, it says, "The heart is deceitful above all things and beyond cure. Who can understand it?" (CEV, 2012) This word deceitful means heart trampled, sick, woeful, having foot traffic from people mistreating it. A mistreated person has a difficult time having a positive attitude towards their life. They expect what the past has given them- more pain, misery and disappointment. Often, they act in a way that provokes a negative, dismissive response from others. (Edwards, 2019)

It can be difficult to forgive a parent who said they were following God but were neglectful or negative in their interactions. It would be hard to separate this model from their view of God or that he has similar behavior and ideas.

The disappointment and anger can seep into their views of God. Their perception of being unlovable and unacceptable even from their creator, can be quite painful. They may conclude that there cannot be any higher power because their rightful human dignity has been denied. People in pain can justify many poor and hurtful actions. Their wounded spirit can make them feel vulnerable and without recourse to improve or change the course of their lives. Proverbs 29:18, "If people can't see what God is doing, they stumble all over themselves." (MSG, 2019)

Financial

In the previously mentioned German study, the no-kiss couples suffered a negative impact financially. The man took home 20 to 30 percent less than his more kissing counterpart. (Bloom & Bloom, 2019)

In the workplace lack of touch can make employees feel unappreciated or undervalued. An employee can respond by not doing their job well, being disruptive, insubordinate and causing overall production to lower. A supervisor with poor relationships to subordinates should refrain from touch. It can be perceived as aggressive and overly controlling.

It is estimated that workplace conflict is responsible for 65 percent of people who lose their jobs, rather than for being incompetence. Inappropriate touch in the workplace can cause an employee to file a grievance and start legal action. Time is lost by employees who discuss the conflict, and additional resources are spent to discipline or replace a distressed team member. The company suffers financial loss due to these workplace disruptions. (Mediation, 2016)

People need love, acceptance and a sense of purpose. Starting with parents, a lack of good touch can cause negative consequences for the human body, emotional well-being, problems in relationships, spiritually depression and negatively impact finances. Workplace can suffer with people feeling wounded, human resource and financial chaos. Temporary loss of affection can affect relationships and cause people to feel rejected and withdraw from others. If you have these symptoms, you may have skin hunger.

Feel Good Now Activity

Get a hairbrush or comb. Give each other a scalp massage and then brush hair. Get a warm washcloth and olive oil. Give your friend a facial by cleaning off their face and then massaging with oil.

* * * *

Acceptance. (n.d.). In Wikipedia. Retrieved April 20, 2019 from https://en.wikipedia.org/wiki/Acceptance

Bloom, L., & Bloom, C. (2019, July 16). Stronger the Broken Places. Https://www.Psychologytoday.Com/. https://www.psychologytoday.com/us/blog/stronger-the-broken-places/201907/kissing-adds-years-your-life

Chillot, R. (2013, March). The Power of Touch.
Https://Www.Psychologytoday.Com/Us/Articles/201303/the-Power-Touch.
https://www.psychologytoday.com/us/articles/201303/the-power-touch

Divecha, D. (2018, October 8). Can a Pregnant Woman's Experience
Influence Her Baby's Temperament?
Http://Www.Developmentalscience.Com/.
http://www.developmentalscience.com/blog/2018/10/1/can-a-pregnant-
womans-experience-influence-her-babys-temperament

Edwards, C. (2018, August 19). Cherie Edwards.
Https://www.Fourcorners.At/. https://www.fourcorners.at/sermons

Fernandez, L., & Matt, S. (2019, June 19). Bored Lonely Angry Stupid Excerpt
Technology Loneliness History. Www.Slate.Com.
https://slate.com/technology/2019/06/bored-lonely-angry-stupid-excerpt-
technology-loneliness-history.html

Goodreads. (n.d.). Eric Liddell Quotes. Https://www.Goodreads.Com/.
Retrieved August 12, 2016, from
https://www.goodreads.com/author/quotes/802465.Eric_Liddell

Gregory, M. (2020, June 16). What Does the "Still Face" Experiment Teach us
about Connection? Https://Psychhelp.Com.Au/.
https://psychhelp.com.au/what-does-the-still-face-experiment-teach-us-about-
connection/

Harmon, E. (2012, February 24). Adoption History: Harry Harlow, Monkey
Love Experiments. Https://Www.Uoregon.Edu/.
https://pages.uoregon.edu/adoption/studies/HarlowMLE.htm

Halton, C. (2020, May 11). Yes, You're smartphone habit is affecting your kids
here's how. Https://Www.Todaysparent.Com/.

https://www.todaysparent.com/family/parenting/yes-your-smartphone-habit-is-affecting-your-kid-heres-how/

James W. Prescott (1975) Body Pleasure and the Origins of Violence, Bulletin of the Atomic Scientists, 31:9, 10-20, DOI: 10.1080/00963402.1975.11458292

Joubert, T. (2013, January 8). US Experiment on Infants Withholding Affection. Https://Stpauls.Vxcommunity.Com/. https://stpauls.vxcommunity.com/Issue/us-experiment-on-infants-withholding-affection/13213

Jones, J. (2018). Why Physical touch matter for your well being. Https://Greatergood.Berkeley.Edu/. https://greatergood.berkeley.edu/article/item/why_physical_touch_matters_for_your_well_being

Mediation Works. (2016). Cost of Conflict Whitepaper. Https://Mediationworks.Com/Wp-Content/Uploads/2016/11/Cost-of-Conflict-Whitepaper-.Pdf. https://mediationworks.com/wp-content/uploads/2016/11/cost-of-conflict-whitepaper-.pdf

Merriam-Webster. (2007). Definition of Love. Http://Wordcentral.Com/. http://wordcentral.com/cgi-bin/student?love

https://www.psychologicalscience.org/publications/observer/obsonline/harlows-classic-studies-revealed-the-importance-of-maternal-contact.html

Verny, T. R., & Weintraub, P. (2003). Pre-Parenting: Nurturing Your Child from Conception. Simon & Schuster.

~~~~

Chapter 4: Analytical Dimensions of Touch

Thai uses the wai to greet each other. The
hands are placed palm side together as if
praying and held near the face as they give a
slight bow. The lower the bow the more respect
is given. (Thai Greeting, n.d.)

Haptics communication is the study of how people express themselves through touch. Researchers have developed different analytical views of describing their ideas. The various types of touch labelled by researchers Heslin & Alper were the five types of touch: Functional/Professional, Social/Polite, Friendship/Warmth, Love/Intimacy, and Sexual Arousal. These permissions of touch between people describe their role in relationships and social settings.

A functional or professional touch is the most formal and occurs in everyday living. Incidental touches occur when purchasing items, going to a health professional, or at work and are a way of completing a task. The touching involved is part of a physical assessment, sharing work assignments, or passing a tool. Incidental touch is done by physicians when they examine a patient by palpitating their abdomen, check inside their ears, take blood pressure, and listen with a stethoscope to the heart and lungs. Touch is essential to perform those tasks. Incidental touches occur without any thought throughout the day.

Greeting handshakes, kisses on the cheek, warm hugs, and pats on the shoulder are Social or Polite touches. These social norms govern touch between men and women. The length and type of handshake communicates social standing. The quantity or placement of kisses depends on personal, cultural, and sexual norms and the age and the current state of the relationship. The kiss may send a message of joy, desire, and friendship.

The touch may be repetitive, reciprocated, or strategic. A repetitive touch may be a series of joyful hugs upon seeing a friend or family member after a long time apart. For an Asian businessman a bow is customary. A Western businessman can return the bow, even if his custom is to greet with a handshake. A strategic touch is used to show one's superiority and exertion of control in the situation. Leadership is demonstrated by shaking hands and then clasping their spare hand on the top of the handshake.

Friendship or warmth is an informal touch. Friend will sit close enough to brush legs, hold hands, stroke hair, pat hands or give a neck rub which offers warmth. In western countries most friendly touch is between female friends. In eastern countries two females or two males will freely display affection. In western countries, touch between men implied either a display of dominance, revealing a man's strength and masculinity or a sexualized meaning. In sports, it is common for teammates to pat another's bottom as encouragement. This same pat in a different context may be interpreted as sexual attraction. In general, in western cultures, men will hug or touch a female more than his male friends. Overall eastern countries, touch between the genders in public is disrespectful. Warm touch is nurturing and offers comfort and support between friends.

As closeness deepens to love, more non-sexual regions of the body are permissible for touch. In relationships with close family or partners, touch barriers are decreased, and physical intimacy increased. Depending on cultural and religious factors, preference, privacy, and desire govern intimate touch. Family time may involve people laying over parent's laps, throwing a leg over a sibling, smacking a sibling's bottom, giving noogies, and playful wrestling, all done in an honoring, friendly or playful way. Close friends may share a bed, do each other's hair and makeup, and give back or foot rubs and comforting hugs.

Sexual relationships honor and respect each one's boundaries and the love of the couple. Expression of love, physical attraction, desire for oneness and the physical and emotional satisfaction of sex are simultaneously experienced. Sexual touch taken outside of this context may feel physically wonderful but incongruent emotionally. The spiritual component is reduced to one individual taking pleasure from another, rather than giving honor through mutual pleasure.

Touch viewed through this lens moves from the outer social interaction circles to the most intimate ones. The touch is appropriate to the relationship between the people and the situation or location they meet. (Haptic, n.d.)

Researcher Elaine Yarbrough studied American non-verbal interactions and observed most touches occurs in non-vulnerable parts of the body. The hand, arm, shoulder and upper back, are non-vulnerable body parts (NVBP), suitable for contact in public settings. The rest of the body, Yarbrough designated as vulnerable body parts (VBP), reserved for close relationships. The VBP region is fit for couples, friends, and private spaces.

In 1985, she and her colleague Stanley Jones divided types of touch into seven distinctions: positive, playful, control, ritual, hybrid, task-related and accidental. The positive touch expressed concern, reassurance, interest and nurturing. This touch is the pat on the back for encouragement, from the coach to a player when she is substituted onto a volleyball team. The child learning to walk will fall in the process. The mother will dust him off, encourage him and positions him to try again. The coach is reassuring her player to do well, while the mother is expressing concern, nurturing and reassurance to her son.

The playful touch is through kindness or aggression to engage physically. Playful aggression is two boys playing superhero and villain. They fight with weapons and end up wrestling to see who is stronger. There is friendliness but a definite assertion of power and craftiness.

The control touch is to cause someone to become aware or follow instructions. When crossing streets, a girl may lightly touch her friend on the arm to alert her to an oncoming car. A teacher will touch a student's shoulder, to bring them to awareness, out of daydreaming and back into a learning mode.

Ritual touch is involved with greetings and departures and the touch that is used between people. In France, French friends will greet each other with three kisses on alternating cheeks. A teacher in the United States may greet his students with a fist bump. The ritual is useful in awareness of culture, relationships and honoring others.

Hybrid is a mix of some of these like a playful hug with a side-to-side swing to say bye to someone. Another mix is a secret handshake for entrance to a treehouse, or club or formal handshake offered that moves into a bear hug and kisses.

Task-related touch is when a doctor examines a patient, a dad picking up a baby to change her diaper, or a firefighter carrying a child to safety. The contact happens as the task is being done.

The accidental touch is unintended, unplanned and often surprising or overlooked. Someone moving through a large crowd may incidentally brush other people. A person may misjudgment of the spatial distance needed to walk past another and bump into them. A salesclerk might touch the hand of the customer while handing over a receipt. Some people may feel uncomfortable or apologetic for bumping into someone else. Usually, both people in the interaction do not view the touch as an attempt to communicate. (Prager, 1997)

Touch can happen incidentally as you cross paths with people during the day. The touch carries different intentions and uses as it happens. There are more public parts of the body where touch can occur by acquaintances. As more emotional intimacy is achieved, people allow casual touch.

Touch can be categorized and described through different lenses to evaluate and process the idea of contact. By using these ideas, a person can see that perhaps touch is happening in their day, but it is not necessarily on purpose and meant to communicate healthy appreciation and affection. These are also some ideas on how touch can naturally happen in a day from intended to incidental.

Feel Good Now Activity

Count how many times that you touch your spouse and kids in the day. When you go to work, how many casual brushes of the hand happen? Watch for the opportunities for touch that go unmet?

* * * *

Haptic. (n.d.). In Wikipedia. Retrieved April 2, 2016 from https://en.wikipedia.org/wiki/Haptic

Jones, Stanley E.; Yarbrough, A. Elaine (2009). "A naturalistic study of the meanings of touch". Communication Monographs. 52 (1): 19–56. doi:10.1080/03637758509376094

Prager, K. J. (1997). The Psychology of Intimacy (The Guilford Series on Personal Relationships) (1st ed.). The Guilford Press.

Thai Greeting. (n.d.). In Wikipedia. Retrieved April 20, 2020 from https://en.wikipedia.org/wiki/Thaigreeting

~~~~~

Mariana M. Brosnan

Chapter 5: Influence Individual Need

Becky and Greg had two daughters. When Izzy was born, she would scream unless she was wrapped tightly in a blanket and held snuggly. Later when her sister, Lupe was born, her parents tried to wrap her tightly. She resisted and cried. She was only content being wrapped loosely in blankets where she could move around and have her arms sticking out. Now the girls are eight and six. They still retain their desire to snuggle, but Izzy prefers being tightly held and Lupe prefers sitting on her dad's lap and having freedom to get up as she wants.

Every individual has a unique desire and critical need for touch. A baby is born with a preset for how much and the quality of touch. As they grow, they will encounter religious and cultural factors, making adaptions to the situations and environment around them.

Personal Settings

Innate touch needs, and desires are scripted into each person's soul and body. Montague describes this picture of a baby exploring touch, as she bumps her own fist into her mouth and feels the pressure of her mom's hand touching her feet when she kicks.

After she is born, she will quickly communicate to her parents, when and how she wants to be held. Some babies liked to have wiggle room while some require their parents to pace the room with them to be soothed. (Montagu, 1971)

In the last chapter, we list the non-vulnerable body parts such as arms where others may touch us. We also have areas on our body where we do not want anyone to touch us, maybe your face or your feet. Another person may not like anyone giving them a hug as it feels vulnerable as they are closed in and for a moment, helpless.

Some variances from culture and personality include: a French friend who danced intimately with many girls as his Austrian girlfriend patiently waited her turn. An Australian guy who laid his head on his female friends' leg to take a rest. A Hungarian girl surprised us that she had been dating a German guy for the last eight months. We had spent a lot of time with them as part of our friend group. They never had any public displays of affection; they never sat or left together, and he never paid for her drink. In my multi-national friend gathering in Vienna, I would hug in greeting with each person. One of my friends was touch-averse and did not like anyone touching him. After a long discussion, in which I talked about needed touch, he agreed that I could respectfully hug him when we met up.

Religious Influences

Each child with their preferences for touch must adapt to the family and religious culture they are born into. Most religions have rules governing touch in families, between friends, members of the same and other religions, medical and service professions and strangers. These rules are designed to ensure models of outward purity and modesty, reflecting inward purity. The rules reinforce the idea that a persons' body belongs to oneself and one's creator. After marriage, it is to be shared in a holy way with their spouse. The rules respect the body, soul and spirit and protect against inappropriate touching.

In the 1600s, religious settlers came from England to America wanting to be independent and live a simple life. The Puritans valued spiritual and familial things and to not distract themselves in impure thoughts. They believed in touch avoidance except between a married man and his wife, and in family warm exchanges. These beliefs were thought to help avoid wickedness and sexual immorality. Even their clothing was plain and modest to not cause unnecessary distraction. Then their attention could be focused on the Judeo-Christian ideas of the importance of hard work, ethical and moral living.

These biblical ideologies were woven in the fabric of life. Infrequent yet clinical touch became the norm in the workplace and in religious meetings. Touch between couples was reduced to only what was necessary for procreation. Puritans were highly encouraged to not hold back their bodies from their spouses and could be granted a divorce if their partner were not able to perform this function. Pursuing religious freedoms and the values of building your own life, Puritans helped lay the groundwork for laws in the American colonies. (Finley, 1995)

The American system has been established on independence and the right to govern your own body. This system has had long-lasting effects in the government and judicial systems. The judicial system has many laws built in to reflect a person's right to your own body and for others to not take advantage of that. Married spouses have a right to each other's body and do not share this special intimate physical relationship outside of their marriage. These protections ensured a human being's right to not be touched and ensure appropriate interactions in families.

Judaism values each person and strives to protect purity. The law prevents touch between unmarried people of the opposite sex, to prevent a step towards a sensual act. For traditionally observant Jews, there is no touching between genders, even a handshake. Close family members can give hugs, kisses and positive touch to each other. Men walking together will often link arms. Women will hug and embrace each other. Professionals can touch the opposite sex within the conduct of their business, such as doctors, hairdressers and emergency workers. By having these standards, sanctity between the sexes is preserved. (Negiah. (n.d.)

In Islam displays of affection between the same sexes is normal. Men will greet with kisses and warm hugs, walk holding hands, walking arm and arm, with an arm around a friend's shoulder. Touch between opposite sexes is reserved for close family. Non-essential touching between people of the opposite sex is prevented to ensure modesty, humility and chastity. Muslims believe in respect and not having physical contact except with close family and friends. Physical touch is given between spouses, ancestors, descendants, sibling and their descendent and aunts and uncles. Public displays of affection between spouses are viewed as tasteless and disrespectful. All people are encouraged to display respect and modesty towards one another.

Religious views of one's body as being holy and respected. Principles are to have respect between the sexes and those outside the family. Honor is given to others. Being in a family, marriage or close friend opens the possibility for loving, appropriate positive touch.

Family Culture

In each family, there are a set of unwritten family rules for how people can interact. The family may be very stoic and not very affirming. A child with higher touch needs may either break all the family rules or try to get their needs met outside their family. If a family if very affectionate, then a family member with less needs and desires for touch may struggle to have comfortable boundaries.

The family may have different rules for inside the home and out. In some families only the parents might kiss each other on the lips while in another family everyone might kiss each other on the lips.

Other rules of touch may be:

Breastfeeding is natural and good but should be done privately.
Dating couples can hold hands while in public.
Married people kiss each other when they say goodbye.

Small children should not climb on adults like they are a tree.
Kiss people on the cheek as a greeting.
Give grandma a kiss.
Don't hug your co-workers. If they are crying or upset just comfort them by a soft touch on the shoulder.
It is ok to sit on Santa's lap.
Adult males can hug small children but need to only do it in public.
Elderly people do not need touch.
The rules of touching may adapt to the gender, age, or situation.
Rules are adjusted as a child grows up and they have interactions outside their family.

Emotional Expression

The English, German, Scandinavian, Chinese, and Japanese cultures use high-emotional restraint. They idealize high-emotional restraint to preserve one's dignity, self-respect and honor. Emotions are regarded as private. Cultural idioms illustrate this restraint ideology, from the British saying "stiff-upper-lip" to the Japanese concept of not displaying or acknowledging strong emotions to "save face." Americans find it demeaning if they are described as "getting emotional" and instruct their sons with "big boys don't cry." Holding strong feelings in demonstrates self-respect and respect for others. Instead of emotional displays, a neutral body posture and facial expressions are adopted. This staunch behavior may be misinterpreted as apathy or implied agreement from the cross-cultural view from more emotionally demonstrative people. (Early & Ang, 2003)

Latinos, Jews, Africans and Middle Easterners have low-emotional restraint cultures. Latinos tend to talk using large gestures. Linguist Deborah Tannen describes Jewish discussions as cooperative overlapping, where the speakers talk at the same time. (Correspondent, 2000) Africans can speak very loudly and with much enthusiasm. Syrians can speak passionately and with intensity to express sincerity.

Each child has personal preferences that are shaped from before they are born. Depending on their family and the gender rules, and norms from religion and culture, the touch needs must conform. They will be influenced and will need to adapt by the emotional expressions of the country they are living in.

Feel Good Now Activity

Ask each member of the family what kind of touch they like, whether a gentle long hug or perhaps a vigorous foot rub and how frequently they prefer it. Find ways to meet touch needs of each person. If you have a touch-avoidant person, ask under what conditions do they like to hug or give touch.

* * * *

Correspondent, J. (2000, May 12). Interrupters: Linguist says it's Jewish way. Jweekly. https://www.jweekly.com/2000/05/12/interrupters-linguist-says-it-s-jewish-way

Early, P., & Ang, S. (2003). Cultural Intelligence: Individual Interactions Across Cultures. Stanford Business Book

Finley, G. (1995). Americans Puritans Today and the "Religious Right." Endtimepilgrim. http://endtimepilgrim.org/puritans13.htm

Montagu, A. (1971). Touching: The Human Significance of the Skin (First Edition). Columbia Univ Pr.

Negiah. (n.d.). In Wikipedia. Retrieved February 23, 2015 from https://en.wikipedia.org/wiki/Negiah

Chapter 6: Memory and Interpretation

An 8-year-old girl received the heart of a 10-year-old girl who had recently passed. The heart transplant recipient started having nightmares of a man coming in her room to attack her. The parents took her to a psychiatrist. After the unusually detailed information from the girl's dreams, the parents contacted the police. The parents found out that the donor had died in an unsolved murder. Their little girl's description led to a murderer. The cells of the heart had imprinted the violent touch along with images of her killer. The man was investigated and DNA evidence tied the man to the crime scene, and he was arrested and convicted. (Joshi, 2011)

Memory Transfer

The skin continuously captures information and stores it in the cells of the body. In the case of organ donors, the memory is transferred in the organ to the recipient. There is documentation from organ recipients how their diets changed, some could recall their donor's memories, like the little heart recipient and one woman changed her sexual orientation.

The donor was a woman who was attracted to men. She donated to a female with same sex attracted attraction. The recipient reported that her attraction for women stopped and she began to be attracted to only men. She is now engaged to marry a man. She states, "I think I got a gender transplant."

Another woman got a donated heart from a teen boy. She suddenly started craving green peppers, beer and chicken nuggets. She was put in contact with the donor's family and found these were all things the young man had loved. (Joshi, 2011)

Biology of Skin

The skin is an amazing organ that receives touch through an electrical impulse and transmits information to the brain. This information is then analyzed and the brain sends a message of how to respond to the input. The different types of receptors in the skin sense pain, emotion, pressure, vibration, texture, chemicals, hot and cold and position of each muscle. This genius system enables people to adapt and stay safe in response to changing stimuli.

Pain receptors called Noci-which is the Latin term for injurious -detect pain or stimuli that can cause damage to the skin or other tissues in the body. There are over three million pain receptors on the skin, in the muscles, bones, blood vessels and certain vital organs. There are three levels of detection: mechanical, like a cut or scrape; thermal stimulation, such as a burn; or chemical, like poison from an insect. The receptors give a sharp pain response to move quickly away from touching a hot pan, or they pulse a dull pain to remind you of an ongoing injury so that healing continues. These receptors give feedback at a speed of sixty miles an hour about environmental factors to avoid. Imagine trying to live without having this vital information! (Lyman, 2020)

The C-tactile fibers receive encoded information about the emotions of the person touching and relay this to the mind. The hairy parts of skin are extremely sensitive to delicate touch. Gently stroking the skin at 2-10 cm/second will cause the brain to release good feelings with serotonin, makes people smile and lowers heart rates. This skin-to-brain communication goes slow by comparison at only two miles an hour and soothes the entire body. (Pawling et all, 2010)

Touch feels good and protects but a researcher wanted to see if emotion could be communicated through touch. A 2009 study at DePauw University focused on whether specific emotions could be communicated only through physical touch. Psychologist Matthew Hertenstein, who conducted the study, recruited strangers to be blindfolded and be touched by another volunteer. Some of these participants had described themselves as low touch with their family and friends. The volunteer had only five-seconds to communicate anger, love, fear, disgust, happiness, sadness, sympathy, and gratitude, without any visual or auditory assistance to the blindfolded intervention. The recipient of the touch correctly identified the intended emotion with a 70 percent accuracy.

Hartstein conducted his study in the U.S., the U.K. and Spain. Frequent touch is part of normal communication in Spain. The Spaniards had an amazing 78 percent accuracy in correctly interpreting the meaning of the touch. (Hertenstein & Keltner, 2009)

Positive aspects of human contact have been done by the Touch Research Institute (TRI) who have conducted more than 100 research studies on the physical and psychological effects of massage on the human body. Their research documented the positive effects of touch as easing pain, improving immune system functioning, decreasing autoimmune problems (such as lupus and arthritis), enhancing alertness, and lowering heart disease risk. (Menehem, 2006)

Studies on massage and medical illnesses have showed positive results. One study on individuals with hypertension who received regular massages showed that this intervention lowered their blood pressure, anxiety, and stress hormones. Massage therapy was also shown to curb migraine headaches. Migraine sufferers received a twice-weekly, 30-minute massage for five consecutive weeks. After the treatment routine, they reported more headache-free days and fewer problems sleeping than the control group. Chronic-headache sufferers reduced weekly headaches as well.

Touch also keeps the immune system more robust. Cancer patients undergoing treatment had a drop in pain level by simply having a loved one hold their hand. It has been shown that massage raises white blood counts, heals scars and raises people's spirits, increasing their chances of survival. In HIV-infected people, massage increased the natural killer cell, fighting tumors and viruses and lowering depression. (Vanderbilt, 2005) Massage brings physical comfort, fortifies the immune system and reduces pain even in childbearing. (Evastar, 2010)

In 1951, French doctor Fernand Lamaze traveled to Russia and observed women giving birth. The women had been educated about the birthing process, given techniques to relax, demonstrated massage on the abdomen, and practiced patterned breathing for labor. These resources helped women to know their experience was normal, helped them keep calm and breath which increased oxygen and lowered pain levels. Based on his research, Lamaze created preparatory classes to educate women about how to cope with the pain of childbirth by using, relaxation breathing, along with a light massage technique that he called effleurage. This circular patterned massage on the abdominal surface helped to sooth a woman in labor, lowering her pain.

In 1965, the Gate Control Theory by Melzack & Wall showed that the pain sensors are smaller than touch receptors. Therefore, by using massage, the labor pains were blocked from sending signals to the brain. This explained why the Lamaze method enabled women to have informed, peaceful and less painful births.

A 1997 Field's research showed that massage could be used to decrease pain and shorten labor and delivery during childbearing. A woman's partner massaged her for 15 minutes each hour. Not only were the feelings of pain decreased, but the labor was shortened by three hours on average. (Field, 2010)

Another effect of touch that has been studied is that aggression increases and cooperation decreases when there is less contact between people. American and French parenting styles were researched to see the correlation between positive touch and aggression. The researchers observed 40 parents and their children in their interaction on playgrounds in the U.S. and France. The Americans touch was primarily corrective and intervening in nature. These children and their parents played and interacted less than their French counterparts. Visual check-ins and physical contact were more frequent between French children and their parents. These children showed superior cooperative ability to play with their peers and demonstrated a less aggressive behavior toward their parents and other children. The study concluded that because of more frequent pleasant touch, the French children were developing a more community-based friendly, attitude towards others. (Field, 1999)

Skin protects us from damage through hot and cold and other harmful touch. Touch is stored in the cells memory to help us avoid those around us with poor intent and keep to friendly people nearby. Humans are extremely sensitive to the emotional communication that is being transmitted. Good touch can help us to reduce pain and feel soothed. There is correlation that having positive touch can cause people to feel less aggressive and enhance community dynamics.

Feel Good Now Activity

Do a massage exchange. Ask your friend to give you a massage for 15 minutes. Find a friend to do massage exchanges together.

* * * *

Evastar. (2010, May 10). The Physical and Physiological Effects of Massage [Online Forum Post]. Digitalworldz.

https://www.digitalworldz.co.uk/threads/the-physical-and-physiological-effects-of-massage.236311/

Fields, T. (2010, March). Pregnancy and Labor. Ncbi.
https://www.ncbi.nlm.nih.gov/pmc/articles/PMC2870995/

Hertenstein, M., & Keltner, D. (2006). Touch Communicated Distinct Emotion. Http://www.Gruberpeplab.Com/Teaching/Psych3131_spring2015/Documents/6.2_Hertenstein_2006_TouchEmotions.Pdf.

Joshi, S. (2011, April 25). Memory Transference in Organ Transplant Recipients. Namahjournal.
https://www.namahjournal.com/doc/Actual/Memory-transference-in-organ-transplant-recipients-vol-19-iss-1.html

Lyman, M. (2020). The Remarkable Life of the Skin: An Intimate Journey Across Our Largest Organ (Illustrated ed.). Atlantic Monthly Press.

Menehem, K. (2006, January). Tiffany Field on Massage Research. Massage Magazine.
https://www.massagemag.com/News/2006/January/125/Tiffany.php

Pawling, R., Cannon, P., McGlone, F., & Walker, S. (2010, March 10). C-Tactile Afferent Stimulating Touch Carries a Positive Value. Ncbi.
https://www.ncbi.nlm.nih.gov/pmc/articles/PMC5345811/

Tiffany Field (1999) Preschoolers in America are Touched Less and are More Aggressive Than Preschoolers in France, Early Child Development and Care, 151:1, 11-17,DOI:10.1080/0300443991510102

Vanderbilt, S. (2005, August). Boosting Immunity Against HIV.Massagetherapy https://www.massagetherapy.com/articles/boosting-immunity-against-hiv

~~~~

Chapter 7: Historical and Clinical Touch

Caesar did not rise off his throne in the Senate to grasp forearms in greeting. Climber pulled Caesar's robe and pulled it back as Casca sunk his knife. The other conspirators struck the next twenty-two strikes. Caesar turned as his friend came at him with a dagger. "E tu, Brute!" he said as he fell dead. (Watson, 2015)

Historical snapshots

As seen in Ancient Egyptian hieroglyphics circa 1800 B.C., the way each man greeted their friends and community members showed relationships and status. Handshakes conveyed power and maintained safety. This formal interaction came from a belief that man could obtain godly power when shaking hands with a god.

In Roman times, men would greet each other by grasping their bared forearms together. This was to ensure one was not carrying a knife to avoid a surprise attack before continuing the meeting. (Andrews, 2020)

We know that there must be a basic level of trust in order to communicate and cooperate with others. People desiring to share information will move to closer proximity, to speak softly or whisper for them to exchange more intimate details. When people desire and move to a close touching distance, sharing of agenda, affection, and intimacy are attainable. When a person deliberately invades someone else's body space, against their wishes, it is perceived as a threat or a show of dominance. People use closeness to show intimacy with their loved ones.

Mariana M. Brosnan

The Victorian era was a time of beauty, purity, and repression. The primary focus was on sexual behaviors and gender roles. Young women were prepared to be stay-at-home wives and mothers. A young woman was never to speak to a man without an accompanying chaperone. Unmarried women were never to have physical contact with men. There was a separation of the spheres in which men and women functioned to have clear boundaries to preserve purity. Touch was only between married partners and in families. It was thought that limiting touch preserved reputation, chastity, and family. (Barrett, 2013)

The need for touch as part of normal child development was first discovered during the nineteenth century. Children abandoned at birth or taken from unfit parents were placed in foundling homes. In these orphanages, the children were properly fed, good hygiene was maintained, and they were protected from danger. Yet the children died, even though their physical needs were being met. Marasmus, a Greek word meaning wasting away, claimed the lives of nearly 100 percent of infants under one year old. (Lakeside Therapeutic, 2016) The foundlings basic need for human physical contact and family bonding was missing and they could not overcome this lack.

By contrast, an infant raised in her own home would be held, intimately cared for, and physically nourished with breastfeeding. Most families slept in a family bed, with everyone together. Children could be cuddled, and babies could easily be fed.

However, poor hygiene and overcrowding with family and neighbors caused any individual who became sick to quickly spread their illness to many around them. These diseases included scarlet fever, whooping cough, chickenpox, mumps, tuberculosis, diphtheria, measles, and rubella. As a result, families aiming to halt the mass spread of diseases gave children less physical interaction and more independence. The connections between the cause and spreading of disease and preventative measures had yet to be discovered.

With the spread of Covid-19, public health measures such as maintaining two-meter distance, not touching our faces or other people and frequent handwashing methods are in place. Keeping people apart seems to help prevent the spreading of colds and viruses.

Influence of Doctors and Behavioral Psychologists

Behavioral psychology is the study and practice of altering people's behaviors, emotions, thoughts and actions. A behavioral theory is developed as a psychologist hypothesizes and studies from their own viewpoint of the psyche. Some psychologists' theories became popular and have shaped ideas of how to create an ideal mature adult.

Early American colonists embraced a spirit of resourcefulness and independence for their children. In 1894, pediatrician Dr. Luther Emmett Holt wrote The Care and Feeding of Children. He believed there was no advantage to holding a child. He instructed parents to give basic, functional touch but not comforting touch. He believed that it was indulgent to pick up a crying child, and the lack of comfort was encouraging the independence of children. He suggested the best solution was to let the child cry it out. This typically involved tolerating the child crying from one to three hours to develop his own self-soothing. Holt also advised giving the child plenty of fresh air by placing her outside in the baby pram or in a window box which were secure wooden boxes hung outside windows.

Other psychologists applied research done in other fields to childrearing. In the 1890s Ivan Pavlov did an experiment on his dog's salivation response. Pavlov had conditioned his dogs to salivate by ringing a bell while feeding them. He then could make them salivate when he rang the bell, but no food was given. This was called a conditioned response.

Behaviorist psychologist founder John B. Watson and his wife, Rosalie Rayner utilized the concept of conditioned response with children. They co-authored Psychological Care of the Infant and Child. They asserted that to grow children into satisfied adults that children should learn to self-soothe their difficulties or needs. Watson believed self-sufficiency would ensure future stable marital relationships, requiring less from their partner and being less "needy."

For this theory to work, they encouraged parents to: "Let your behavior always be objective and kindly firm. Never hug and kiss (the children), never let them sit in your lap. If you must, kiss them once on the forehead when they say goodnight. Shake hands with them in the morning. Give them a pat on the head if they have made an extraordinarily good job of a difficult task." Watson's child-rearing ideas put away previous romanticism of children to embrace the newly emerging science and technological developments of the 1950s. (Bigelow & Morris, 2001)

Medical and parenting guru Dr. Spock wrote Baby and Childcare in 1946. The book quickly became a best seller with 750,000 copies sold. Spock encouraged parents to teach their children to comfort themselves. Parent's natural instincts were disregarded as primitive and uneducated. The parent's objections could not be defended against the new scientific research and public's embrace of modern practices. This culturally dominant thought of encouraging independence and minimizing intervention was believed to create a secure child. This hands-off approach prevailed over previous ideas of comfort for children.

Not every behavioral researcher of this scientifically driven era agreed with this independence-based philosophy. In 1929, Goodspeed & Johnson explained that if a child is given affection, she will not be seeking outside her family to have her touch needs met. Groves & Groves, 1924, concurred that babies and children need "affection and stability, moderate love that flows gently on throughout their childhood," for their mental and physical needs to be met.

Clinical touch

The diagnostic benefit of medicinal touch has been apparent for twenty-five centuries since the Greeks in 460 B.C. documented palpation-touch for diagnosis. The physician interviews the patient about their health history, gives a visual examination, checks the urine and spit. She then examines the ailing body through touch and listening for health or disease in vital organs. (Hajar, 2018)

A healer could identify, through touching their patient's body and feeling for abnormalities, what symptoms were normal, and which needed further medical intervention. The exam could help to determine illnesses, lumps, broken bones, soft or hard spots, rashes, fever, chills, and reflex-reactions by the power of knowledgeable touch. Women were guided through pregnancy, labor, and childbirth, as their midwife or doctor monitored fetal position by touching the abdomen. The wisdom gained of a healthy versus an ill body could be passed down through successive healers. They could find symptoms and identify the root of a problem. They could try treatments and cures such as medicinal or herbal remedies and vouch for their effectiveness. Touch was used to track the course of treatment for their validity.

Cooperative touch is essential for humans to interact. The understanding of how important touch is for child development has grown through trial and error, psychological research, and clinical touch to diagnose and treat patients. The process of gathering of vital information of health and illness in the body is relayed to the next generation of healers by instructive physical touch.

When Dr. Sigmund Freud began psychoanalysis theory, he believed all human behavior was driven by human sexual and infantile drives. He refused to touch his patients. His method would involve him sitting behind his patients, who were lying on a couch. Freud would ask questions to identify his patient's problem. He believed that any touch between doctor and client would gratify these immature drives. As the head of International Psychoanalytical Association, (IPA), Freud prohibited doctor-patient touch with his colleagues in their practices. He believed if people could resolve their childhood traumas, they would become responsible adults. (Zur & Nordmarken, n.d.)

It has been demonstrated that using a supportive touch gesture increases dopamine and aids people in coming out of depressive states. Hunter & Struve theorized and showed how a therapist can help a patient in issues of the past and coping with the present when nurturing touch is involved in the therapy.

Historically, touch has been given a lesser or more important role in the development of children and in healthy adults at various points in time. Popular trends have outweighed parents' own feelings. In the field of medicine, palpation has been a reliable diagnostic tool. Although many of Freud's theories have been debunked, there is still controversy over whether there should be touch between psychotherapist and their patients. Some doctors believe that a patient-led touch, such as a handshake or a hug is the most compassionate way to support a patient.

Feel Good Now Activity

Practice giving firm handshake. Stand up, extending your right hand and keep your thumb up. Clasp hands and wrap fingers around theirs and pump one or two times. Let go and give a smile. Do not keep your hand floppy like a limp fish nor use all your force to crush the other person's hand.

* * * *

Andrews, E. (2020, March 16). What is the Origin of the Handshake. History. https://www.history.com/news/what-is-the-origin-of-the-handshake

Barrett, K. (2013). Victorian Women and Their Working Roles. Available from http://www.digitalcommons.buffalostate.edu/ 5-2013

Bigelow, K. M., & Morris, E. K. (2001). John B. Watson's advice on child rearing: Some historical context. Behavioral Development Bulletin, 10(1), 26-30. http://dx.doi.org/10.1037/h0100479

Hajar R. (2018). The Pulse in Ancient Medicine Part 1. Heart views : the official journal of the Gulf Heart Association, 19(1), 36–43. https://doi.org/10.4103/HEARTVIEWS.HEARTVIEWS_23_18

Holt, L. E. (2008). The Care And Feeding Of Children: A Catechism For The Use Of Mothers And Children's Nurses (1909). Kessinger Publishing, LLC.

Hunter, M. G., & Struve, J. (1998). The Ethical Use of Touch in Psychotherapy (And Political Culture). SAGE Publications, Inc.

Lakeside Therapeutic. (2016, January). The Incredible Importance of Touch for Babies. https://lakesidelink.com/blog/lakeside/the-incredible-importance-of-touch-for-babies/

M.D., S. B., & M.D., N. R. (2011). Dr. Spock's Baby and Child Care: 9th Edition (9th ed.). Pocket Books.

Wason, D. (2015, May 15). The Murder of Julius Caesar. Ancient.Eu/. https://www.ancient.eu/article/803/the-murder-of-julius-caesar/

Watson, J. (1928). Psychological Care of Infant and Child. Unwin Brothers.

Why Marriage Matters 26 Conclusions from the Social Sciences. (n.d.). http://www.Familyscholars.Com. Retrieved July 12, 2019, from

Mariana M. Brosnan

https://cdn.shopify.com/s/files/1/0275/9135/files/Why-Marriage-Matters.pdf?3573788516863415290

Zur, O., & Nordmarken, N. (n.d.). To Touch or Not To Touch: Exploring the Myth of Prohibition On Touch In Psychotherapy And Counseling. Zurinstitute /. Retrieved September 1, 2020, from https://www.zurinstitute.com/touch-in-therapy

~~~~

Chapter 8: Remarkable Stories of Positive Touch

There is a beach volleyball court in downtown Kailua Kona, Hawaii. I observed a game of two-on-two volleyball. The team that scored steady points, constantly slapped hands after each play. Regardless of making a good serve, scored a point or were scored on, they would slap hands to either celebrate or encourage each other. The opposite team only slapped hands if they scored a point or occasionally if the other team hit the ball out of bounds. The team with the most physical contact won.

After a short break, one player on each team switched sides. I quickly figured out who was the instigator of the touch. He began to celebrate with his new teammate, one of the guys he had just beaten. On the other side of the net, the guy who had previously been part of the winning team, tried to bring the tradition of slapping hands for encouragement and as celebration. His teammate would not touch hands unless they scored a point. The man who was a natural initiator of the hand slap could pair with any

player and activate them to win. It was an

upward reward and winning cycle he could

establish with his teammate.

Virginia Satir, a respected family therapist, believed in the continued physical exchange between people. She famously said, "We need four hugs a day for survival. We need eight hugs a day for maintenance. We need twelve hugs a day for growth." Her natural down-to-earth way of interacting and building trust to give comfort, gave her a valuable reputation and many people became followers of her style. (Simon, 2018)

The human body, with its many nerve endings covering the skin, is ready for touch. The positive effects of touch on body, mind, spirit and soul promote good self-esteem and kindness to others. The benefits are physical, emotional, mental, spiritual and even financial well-being. In some instances, touch has even helped revive the dead.

Physical Benefits

From eight-weeks of fetal development, the developing infant gives and receives touch. He responds to the touch of his own body, the uterus walls, and the touch of his mother, his father and family. As his life outside the womb begins, he fortifies his immune system by breastfeeding, and he enjoys the stimulus of the skin-to-skin connection.

A 1950's study done on primates demonstrated that emotional connection did not necessarily correlate to the activity of being fed. Infant Rhesus monkeys were placed between two sorts of mothers. One was a hard-wire cage with a bottle and the other was wire-cage covered with a soft blanket. The monkeys would drink from the bottle but immediately return and cuddle the blanket-covered mother. If the monkey were startled, he would quickly get to the blanket and stroke it to comfort himself. The monkey did not feel comforted or try to draw nurturing by the wire mother who simply feed him. (Psychological Science, 2018)

The University of Cambridge researched how eye contact affects babies. When the mother and her child eyes lock, their brain activity synchronizes. The child sees that the mother has time and attempts to verbalize to communicate. (University, 2017)

Standard care for premature infants involves the mother or father with their infant skin-to-skin. Termed kangaroo care, this stimulates lung development, stabilizes breathing, body temperature and heart rates, increases the possibility of breastfeeding, lowers mortality rates and shortens hospital stays and even played a role in reviving a premature infant.

In 2010, David and Kate Ogg, an Australian couple from Queensland, gave birth prematurely to their twins at 27 weeks. The doctor examined the twins and told them that the female twin was stable, but the male twin would not survive. Kate insisted on holding him against her and his father's bare chest. The parents kept their son warm, told him about the life they had planned for him and mourned what would not be. The boy started breathing normally and grasped his dad's finger. The parents requested that the doctor check again, but he refused. He told them any signs of life were part of the dying process.

Finally, the parents said they agreed their son would not live and asked for the doctor for an examine. Upon arriving, the doctor realized the vital signs had stabilized and gave the infant immediate care. Kate and David realized that the power of touch saved their son. They have continued to give frequent physical connection to their son and daughter, who are now happy, healthy ten-year-old's. (Crane, 2015)

Doulas and midwives ease a woman's delivery process by giving valuable massage to decrease pain. They also give verbal encouragement and comfort measures to make labor quicker and delivery less stressful. With effleurage or other types of massage, pain receptors are overridden by the pleasure messages delivered to the mother's brain, interrupting and decreasing the pain. Massage has the additional benefit of increasing blood circulation, helping the laboring mother relax physically and feel supported emotionally.

Labor and delivery nurses are trained on the healing touch of kangaroo care. A quick-acting nurse in North Carolina used the principles in reverse, to have the newborn help revive its own mother. In 2014, Shelly Cawley was given an emergency Cesarean to deliver her daughter Rylan. Shelly had toxemia and went into a coma. She did not come out of anesthesia and the doctors did not think she would live through the night. The nurses placed the newborn, just in a diaper, on her mom's bare chest. The baby slept for about ten minutes, while the nurse and dad tried to wake her up, before letting out a cry. Shelly's vital statistics responded and ten days later she came out of the coma to meet Rylan for the first time. Both baby and mother are in good health without any negative lasting effects. (Bever, 2015)

Positive touch works not only on the young but maintains health and emotional stability in adulthood. A German research study found that a husband who kissed his wife daily, has his life extended by five years. It is not only the act of kissing but the overall emotional connection and reduced stress that has a positive influence. Couples having sex one to two times a week produce 30 percent more IgA, an infection-fighting immunoglobulin that increases resistance to colds and other illnesses and diseases. The increased skin-to-skin contact promotes health and emotional well-being. (Emery, 2015)

Mental and Emotional Well-Being

Hugging increases the hormone oxytocin, nature's happy pill, and causes our bodies to relax. An optimal 20-second-long hug lowers stress, blood pressure and heart rate. The body floods the brain with dopamine, the natural feel-good drug, and increases serotonin levels in the brain, pushing away depression and increasing joyful moods. (Enell, 2019)

These emotions start for babies in the womb. She experiences joy, love and acceptance causing her to feel secure.

Born without the ability to survive on her own, she depends on her parents. Developmental psychologist Sharon Heller states that as her needs are met, she feels secure attachment to her parents.

She views herself and her mother as one unit for the nine months following birth. Her sense of control over her mother's body to be warm, fed, cuddled, treated gently makes her emotions stable and peaceful. With her basic need met, her sense of physiological survival is ensured, and she can move onto learning and developing.

The child's brain is physiologically enhanced through the nurturing relationship with her mother. The hippocampus region of the brain controls learning, memory, and stress response. When she has a secure attachment to her mother, the activity in the hippocampus is well-regulated, and the child's ability to choose calm responses is enhanced by ten percent.

A secure child will be fortified against insecurities, dysfunctions, emotional defense systems or selfishness. He can form close bonds without fear and enjoy a peaceful, healthy, and long life with positive, intimate relationships. "One who feels in control is less likely to commit acts of violence, will have fewer physical problems, and live longer." (Heller, 1997).

The mother, father and baby all experience bonding through caregiving touch. The parents experience the same colorful positive thrill in their interactions as she will. The more contact and touches, the more reinforcement of love and acceptance are passed along to all those in the relationships.

Positive touch brings a surge of emotions. It feels wonderful and affirming to be touched by caring people in our lives. Dacher Keltner, UC Berkley psychologist professor, cites the work of neuroscientist Edmund Ross, who found that physical touch activates the brain's orbitofrontal cortex, which is linked to feelings of reward and compassion. Keltner contends that "studies show that touch signals safety and trust, it soothes. It activates the body's Vagus nerve, the interface of the parasympathetic control of the heart and digestive tract. The nerve is intimately involved with our compassion response and a simple touch can trigger release of oxytocin, aka "the love hormone." This bonding hormone causes people to feel secure and trusting. Touch lowers anxiety and depression, hyperactivity, inattentiveness and stress hormones. (Kraus & Keltner, 2010)

Consistent positive touch makes a person more resistant to abusive touch. Children who have the base knowledge of positive touch can more quickly detect damaging touch. They know that touch with visceral, physical, emotional or spiritual negative feelings is easily identified and avoided.

I loved being hugged and getting back rubs from my dad. He was always respectful in touch towards me. In our town, an adult male friend of my parents would greet me and my younger sisters with a hug. He was from a respected family, a religious married man, with two young sons. Once when he hugged me, I viscerally felt something was "off" about him and I did not like his touch. I told my mom that he could no longer hug me or my little sisters. My mom asked if he had done something offensive. I said no but that there would be no more hugs from him to us. If he attempted to hug me, I would not let him. I would also stand in between him and my sisters and not let him touch us. About twenty years later, we found out that around this time he molested girls who were our same age. I was glad I had followed my intuition and spared myself and my sisters. I believe that because of my many positive touches, I could sense that something was wrong and avoided becoming a victim and saved my sisters too.

Beyond being able to defend against possible negative touch, affirming touch can lower aggressive behavior. A study done among teens in France and teens in the U.S., showed higher friendliness and cooperativeness in France, a higher-touch culture. The French teens were demonstrative in their touch. Both guys and girls would lean on each other, rub each other's backs or hang an arm around each other, with both their same-sex and opposite-sex peers.

In contrast, American teens were less likely to touch their peers in any positive way. They gave themselves positive touch through rubbing their own arms or wrapping their arms around themselves. These teens engaged in more aggressive behavior and speech with their peers. The correlation showed the more positive touch, the less aggressive the teen's communication and interactions became. (Wright, 2020)

Spiritually

In Jesus' time, there were people suffering from a disease called leprosy, which eats away at the skin and is very contagious. (Nepal, 2020) Once leprosy was diagnosed, the infected person would leave their village to live in a cave. They had to yell out, "Unclean, unclean" wherever they went. This prevented people from accidentally touching them and catching their disease or at least become ceremonially unclean according to Jewish law. No one would touch them, and the lepers had to survive by begging. In Mark 1:40 and 41, a leper comes to Jesus and "begged, "You have the power to make me well, if only you wanted to." Jesus felt sorry for the man. He put his hand on him and said, "I want to! Now you are well." At once the man's leprosy disappeared, and he was well." (CEV Holy Bible) When Jesus touched the leper, Jesus would then be made unclean under the law. Instead, Jesus made the man clean. The man was healed emotionally and spiritually because he believed and was totally healed through Jesus' touch.

Another healing through touch is recorded in Matthew 9th chapter. A woman had a bleeding condition for 12 years and had not gotten any help from doctors. In her society she was considered unclean. She had faith that if she could just touch Jesus' clothes she would be healed. She was immediately healed, and Jesus recognized that power had gone out from him. Her faith accessed the healing.

There are many recorded stories in the Bible and in our present day of physical and emotional healings. Followers of Jesus are told to lay hands on the sick and they will recover. I have personally been a part of praying for people and laying my hands on them and seeing people be healed physically and emotionally.

Financial Benefits

Human contact can increase daily financial success by enhancing productivity in companies, increasing a waiter's tip or helping an NBA teams play more effectively.

A study conducted in 1998 looked at whether waitstaff touching customers affected the tip. Both male and female diners responded by increasing the money they tipped. When a waitress was able to convey caring feelings, the gratitude jumped by 36 percent. Younger customers were more influenced to increase their tip than older people. (Lynn & Sherwyn, 1998)

In the workforce, a boss with good employee relationships can increase productivity if he politely touches them on their arms or shoulders. This contact in the course of work environments conveys the boss's approval and the subordinate mirrors back by being a more collaborative, agreeable productive worker. This positive touch can extend to coworkers, subordinates and customers. The higher-ranking individual must initiate the touch for this to be effective. A subordinate's casual touch to a superior can communicate lack of respect. (Let their words, 2012)

German men who kissed their wives before leaving for work had a financial benefit. These men earned 20-30 percent more than the men who did not kiss. The affectionate men had more congenial relationships and these peaceful, cooperative relationship were reflected by success in the workplace.

A study on the relationship between frequency of touch and on-court success was conducted in the NBA by Keltner, Haung & Kraus. Each NBA team's success was documented from pre-season to the championship. Individual members of a team were tracked on how many positive touches they gave each other during play. The count was based on specific criteria. A touch was measured when touch occurred from fist bumps, high 5's, chest bumps, leaping, shoulder bumps, chest punches, head slaps, head grabs, low 5's, high ten's, full hugs, half hugs and team huddles.

"We were very surprised. Touch predicted performance across all the NBA teams," says Kraus. It did not matter where the team ranked, what salary a player had or their position played, the teams who won positively reinforced each other after a play. Incredibly, within 600 milliseconds of scoring a basket, the player received four touches on average from their teammates to celebrate.

The teams with the least amount of contact ranked at the bottom. Touch reinforcement to team success became a positive spiral that increased cooperation and successes, reaping more positive contact. (Kraus & Keltner, 2010)

Human contact is essential and vital to a whole person. Touch keeps people well and regulates vital organs producing good health in the body. This release of happiness fills the mind and uplifts the emotions. Healing of the body and mind can happen with physical touch. Financial reward increases as we give respectful touch to workmates or teammates. Positive touch is free tool to invigorate your whole life.

Feel Good Now Activity

Give everyone in your house a kiss as they or

you exit and enter the house. If you live alone,

find a mirror to give yourself a smooch or your

dog or a soft toy a squeeze.

* * * *

Bever, L. (2015, September 17). The incredible story of how a newborn's cry may have helped save her mother's life. Washingtonpost
https://www.washingtonpost.com/news/to-your-health/wp/2015/09/16/the-

incredible-story-of-how-a-newborns-cry-may-have-helped-save-her-mothers-life/?noredirect=on&utm_term=.0e453684349d

Crane, E. (2015, March 13). Revived by the Power of Love. Dailymail. https://www.dailymail.co.uk/news/article-2992862/The-miracle-baby-born-three-months-early-written-doctors-brought-life-mother-s-touch-five-years-old-s-never-sick.html

Emery, L. (2015, December 1). The Effect Sex Has On Your Immune System. Bustle. https://www.bustle.com/articles/123061-the-one-surprising-effect-sex-has-on-your-immune-system

Enell. (2019, May 24). Embrace the 20 Second Hug for Better Health. Https://Enell.Com/. https://enell.com/blogs/blog/embrace-the-20-second-hug-for-better-health#:~:text=During%20a%20hug%2C%20we%20release,are%20good%20for%20your%20heart!

Heller, S. (1997). The Vital Touch (1st ed.). Holt Paperbacks.

Kraus, M. W., Huang, C., & Keltner, D. (2010). Tactile communication, cooperation, and performance: An ethological study of the NBA. Emotion, 10(5), 745–749 https://doi.org/10.1037/a0019382

Let Their Words Do the Talking. (2012, July). Psychologytoday. https://www.psychologytoday.com/us/blog/let-their-words-do-the-talking/201207/six-tips-get-higher-tips

Lynn, M., Le, J., & Sherwyn, D. (1998). Reach Out and Touch Your Customers. Https://Scholarship.Sha.Cornell.Edu/. https://scholarship.sha.cornell.edu/cgi/viewcontent.cgi?article=1111&context=articles

Nepal Leprosy Trust. (2020). Biblical Leprosy. Nlt.Org
https://www.nlt.org.uk/about/biblical-
leprosy/#:~:text=Although%2C%20as%20mentioned%20above%2C%20mod
ern,of%20leprosy%20in%20the%20Bible

Psychological Science. (2018, June 20). Harlow's Classic Studies Reveal the
Importance of Maternal Contact. Https://Www.Psychologicalscience.Org/.

Simon, R. (2018, February 22). The Healing Touch of Virginia Satir.
Https://Awaken.Com/2018/02/the-Healing-Touch-of-Virginia-Satir/.
https://awaken.com/2018/02/the-healing-touch-of-virginia-satir/

University of Cambridge. (2017, November 17). Eye Contact with your Baby
helps Synchronise Your Brainwaves. Cam.Ac /.
https://www.cam.ac.uk/research/news/eye-contact-with-your-baby-helps-
synchronise-your-brainwaves

Wright, J. (2020, April 17). What Happens When We Can't Touch Each
Other? Skin Hunger.Refinery29. https://www.refinery29.com/en-
us/2020/04/9694663/what-is-skin-hunger-people-touching-contact

~~~~

Mariana M. Brosnan

Section Two:

Guide to Solving

the Skin Hunger Crisis

Mariana M. Brosnan

Chapter 9: Be Ready For Contact

Carol is a chiropractor who helps heal people. She has trained using techniques with touch to sense an imbalance in the body. I had been in a car accident and had torn ligaments in my shoulder. After several months I still had aches and pains from having to adapt my sleep position. At our appointments, Carol would always greet me with a light, comforting hug. I would tell her what part of my body was in the most pain. She placed her hands on this muscle group and try different approaches to resolve the pain.

Sometimes she would rub both ends of a muscle where they connected into the bone. For example, my forearm hurt, so she would massage the elbow and wrist where the muscle inserted. Other times, when my pelvis was twisted and one side rotated forward, she would make an adjustment to the bones and sense if the body responded positively or not. Most of the time, the pain would rapidly decrease or stop if it were the correct diagnosis, and other times the pain would remain the same or increase if it was

not the correct direction. After the appointment,

we would hug again. I believe much healing

came through her medically knowledgeable

hands. I am living pain-free on most days and

with stretching keep my body balanced.

Readiness

   Determine your own readiness to incorporate more touch in your life. Some changes can be implemented immediately or over time. Here are some questions to self-evaluate:
Are there other major events taking place in your life currently?

Do you have energy and time to address any underlying issues of why you have not had sufficient touch?

Are you willing to change old attitudes?

Are you committed to having more physical contact with appropriate family and friends?

What are your motivations for giving and receiving more touch in your life?

Do you understand the adjustment for you and those around you?

Can you respond with kindness if someone refuses to allow touch?

Can you respect another person's process of adapting in touch?

Are you willing to seek out more touchy people or to use professional resources on your way to incorporate more touch in your life?

Take some time and assess your life. This takes a snapshot of who you are and what changes you believe are necessary. You can decide to start to enjoy affection from others. With some consistent practice, you will increase your natural touch benefits.

Forgiveness

You may have suffered from neglect or abusive touch. These past incidents that have not been addressed can dictate how you interact today. These memories can affect your current decisions and you will need to resolve them to have a better future. Parents, caregivers, or siblings are the usual culprits who have neglected or abused you as a child. (Puder, 2019)

Blame and guilt are the two side of a scale which try to maintain balance in your conscience. Blame is holding onto the wrongs done against you. It keeps a list and weight of the injuries someone did that hurt you. You can use these to justify doing bad things against them or someone else. Guilt is the bad feeling for your responses towards those who hurt you or the wrong things you have done. When you choose to forgive the ones who hurt you, the weight on the blame side of the scale is removed. This is when the full weight of guilt can be felt in the conscience. Sometimes it feels easier instead of facing what we have done as wrong and forgiving ourselves, we will sometimes "pick up" the blame again to rebalance the scales.

For example, older and stronger brother Rick is wrestling with his younger brother Dave. Rick is not being careful but accidentally ends up injuring his brother. Dave punches his brother in the gut and calls him a jerk. Dave blames Rick for hurting him. He feels some guilt for his reaction, but he knows his brother started it. Dave will have to forgive Rick for unintentionally hurting him and ask forgiveness for his poor response. If he can no way to speak to Rick (perhaps he has died), Dave can still repent from his own behavior and forgive his brother and reap the positive benefits.

These two parts, forgiving and repenting, will unravel the negative emotion and bitterness from the incident. It is important to forgive others and yourself for all the painful and damaging emotions. By addressing both sides of the situation, you can be free of all the pain to move free of this incident. It may take some time and you may need to remind yourself that you have addressed this incident until it no longer feels painful.

Make a list of the people who have hurt you or of your own hurtful responses. Be sure to include any situations in which touch was involved. There may have been inappropriate touch or neglect for another person's touch needs. Address each situation that comes to mind. If you have previously addressed something, and it feels resolved, it is important you do not rehash it. Forgive the offender and forgive yourself as needed. When you have off-loaded the blame and guilt from your life, you may experience a feeling of being physically lighter. When you do not have to work against a backlog of negative or neglectful experiences, you can be open to more possibilities to have positive, loving touches with others.

Assess your own touch needs

Here is a list of questions to assess what your needs are:
What are your personal non-sexual touch needs and desires?

Are you honoring your commitments to God, yourself or others when pursuing your touch needs?

Do your needs break any religious, legal, moral, ethical, societal, hierarchy rules that you need to keep in mind?

Depending on your age, gender, religion, socioeconomic status, or occupation there will be different societal norms for touch.?

What is your goal of getting more touch?

Do you have a spouse or children or friends that you wish to have more loving touch with?

What kind of meaningful touch situations do you envision having?

What kinds of exchanges do you feel have been missing that you want to incorporate to your life?

If you are single, then who can you plan to interact with in a positive way?

Relationship guides

With your immediate or extended family, create a greeting with hugs and kisses. Sit in closer proximity to your friends so you can touch them while speaking. Think about what emotions you wish to convey with your words and touch.

If you are single, let your family and friends know that you desire more touch, hugs and physical comfort in your life. Often, people have at least one super-touchy friend, that they can always count on for giving them an exuberant hug. Ask the hugger for a long embrace when you meet.

With your co-workers, friends, family or social groups gradually increase meaningful touch with them. Be intentional by doing things, such as patting co-worker on back while speaking to her. Greet people with a warm handshake and put your other hand on top, while smiling and saying, "It is really great to meet you!"

With people that you have a safe friendship, depending on the comfort level of both people, offer to give them neck rub, head rub, shoulder or back rub. While playing sports, give your teammates high-5's and fist bumps. Take a dance class or a couple's exercise class to get lots of good touches and have fun.

Join activities and sports that involve touching such as volleyball, basketball, dancing and painting pictures. Incorporate touch into the interactions as you build the team spirit. The touch will feel good in the visceral and physical way in the anticipation, actual touch and remembrance of the touch.

Be attentive to friends who say they have a backache or headache. Ask them if they would like a massage. Get some olive oil and give them a 10–15-minute massage. Older people may enjoy having their foot or hand lightly massaged. The gentle pressure will improve blood circulation, leave them feeling great and help avoid bruising.

If you are in a romantic relationship, add more non-sexual affection. Hold hands when walking or watching a movie together. Offer a supportive touch when the other is doing a task, such as patting their shoulder or giving a kiss. Sit close to each other to have opportunities to physically connect with each other. When talking over a meal, give eye contact and touch their arm to express emotional support.

If you are suddenly single again, after a romance ending, it is a critical time to find other ways to get hugs and emotional needs met. If you are high-touch, volunteer to give a friend a massage or hold babies that are drug-detoxing in the hospital. You could host friends over for a slumber party-movie watching night or get a job as a professional cuddler. Ask if you can come over and help a family with small children. Usually, you will be covered with dirt and fingerprints and hugs. By meeting someone else's need for touch, you can meet your own.

Professional/group help

Nearly 12 Billion dollars were spent in the United States in 2013 on comfort and health professionals. Chiropractors, massage therapists and acupuncturists are medically trained in how to get tight muscles to relax and leave the body feeling good. Chiropractors give massages and manipulate the bones. They can rub sore areas, allowing muscles to loosen up and more freedom of movement. Having regular massage visits is an opportunity to get lots of skin-to-skin touches and to work out emotional and physical knots from stress. An acupuncturist will use touch to place the needles in key spots. They have knowledge of pressure points and finding a way to relieve stress and tension.

Alternative medicine professionals in different disciplines can add more soothing touch into your life. They can help bridge to feeling more comfortable with touching others.

In chapter 14, there are other resources if you feel you need more help from a trained counselor or psychologist.

Adding more physical touch to your life is not difficult. First address any neglect or negative touch memories from the past and aware of your own touch needs and desires. Engage touchy friends and professionals, whose job is giving touch, to meet touch needs.

Feel Good Now Activity

Find ten different items with varying textures and fabrics, like feathers, buttons, knit hat and leather shoes. Rub your fingertips on them and discover what are the different sensations. Pay attention to see what other types of things you touch today.

* * * *

Puder, D. (2019, April 11). The Science Behind Forgiveness and How it Affects Our Mental Health. Https://Www.Psychiatrypodcast.Com/. https://www.psychiatrypodcast.com/psychiatry-psychotherapy-podcast/2019/4/10/what-is-forgiveness

~~~~

Mariana M. Brosnan

Chapter 10: Guide To A Lifetime Of Good Touch

Graham walked into the room where his friends Henry and Ann were talking. Graham immediately sensed Ann's fallen mood and drawn face. He sat on the couch next to her touching her with his shoulder, arm, and leg. He did not say much but began talking to Henry. In about five minutes, Graham sensed Ann's mood had brightened and he adjusted his body away from his contact with her. Henry commented on how just the touch had been enough to bring a change in Ann's emotions.

Daily affirmative touch is necessary throughout the lifespan. People often forgo contact unless they are in a happy, healthy, loving relationship. The value of physical contact between adults can be overlooked. Sometime people want to make sure that their affection is received so they exaggerate with a long embrace and sway. Because it is essential to everyone, it is important to develop good touch habits. Engage others with hugs, kisses on cheeks, pats on the back and arms, supportive touches on the shoulder.

Positive touch is what feels good, both from the giver and the receiver's perspectives. This non-sexual touch affirms the body and soul. The touch encompasses a physical, emotional, spiritual, and visceral experience. The anticipation, actual experience, and the memory should all feel good and age appropriate. Touch that is appropriate to relationship boundaries honors the soul and spirit.

In anticipation of the touch, the body and soul are open to this experience, between these individuals. During the touch, a pleasant, peaceful feeling is experienced. The exchange is not awkward or disturbing and does not leave behind an uncomfortable visceral feeling. After the touch, the recollection of the time continues to be experienced as positive and not confusing.

The physical touch should fit the relationship status, be age-appropriate, considerate of the time spent, aware of the environment and situationally appropriate. It should be able to be witnessed as innocent and respectful. It should not violate moral, ethical, or legal codes between humans. Touch is positive when it is safe in honoring the people involved. Positive touch feels great and reinforces love and acceptance between people.

> *"The difference between what we do and we*
>
> *are capable of doing would suffice to solve most*
>
> *the of the world's problems." (Mahatma Gandhi)*

Good Touch Throughout the Lifespan

Pre-birth

Touch is the first way a developing fetus communicates with his mother. When he is gently patted, he leans into her hand to touch her back. He already prefers positive, soothing touch. Affirmation and acceptance cross from one to the other. He moves away from any rough or hard touch.

A mother and father can interact with their growing fetus by talking to the baby and applying soft pressure on the pregnant woman's abdomen. The mom can wear looser fitting clothes that are comfortable and not restraining. The mom and dad can work to be peaceful so that the child experiences a less stressed environment. Pregnant moms can be busy but also need to mentally acknowledge their child and give warm pressure or feel her tummy when her baby move, has hiccups or pushes its foot out.

A child born vaginally gets a vigorous all-over-body hug, as he passes through the birth canal. His alertness is higher than Caesarean-born babies, who have lower active times and a higher response to stimulus in the first six days following their births.

Newborn to Infant

God's design and a mother's intuition to nurse him give him the skin-to-skin contact that is more vital to development than breast milk nutrients. Researchers have found that propping an infant's bottle up for feeding withdraws all the benefits of bonding. Breastfeeding is optimal for his growth, survival, and success. Where breastfeeding is not possible, skin-to-skin contact is recommended to give the benefit of physical touch support.

Newborn infant massage can give pleasant stimulation to the baby's skin while bonding the parents to their child. The father can gently rub his daughter's back and legs, while holding her supported on his chest. Some parents claim massage helps a baby sleep better, lessens gas and is just super enjoyable.

When an infant feels a parent's frustration or extreme fatigue, he may become unable to the soothed. The baby senses and feed off his parent's stress. The other parent or another person who comes in a peaceful mood, transmitting peace can get the baby to suddenly stop crying. By displaying soothing energy, the parent conveys calm and her baby mirrors back the feelings.

In Japanese culture, the baby benefits from constant contact with her mother, called skin-ship. She is carried skin-to-skin with her mother, breastfeeds on demand, co-sleeps, enjoys infant massage, and is carried on her mother's back. The baby can easily be calmed because she can hear the familiar sounds of her mother's heartbeat, respiratory and digestive system. The mother and her baby communicate through their non-stop skin interaction. The skin-ship is carried over to the co-sleeping arrangement. The child will sleep on mats with parents through teen years and this may also include the grandparents. The family members contact during close sleeping arrangements reinforces bonding and protection in the family. (McKenna, 2007)

Toddlers

A toddler learning to walk will use his mother as safe place. When he has had sufficient affirmation, he will feel confident to explore the world. If he gets hurt or gets hungry, he knows he can return to mom's arms and ask for help, food, cuddling and get put to sleep. Positive touch is included in daily care and play. The routines of by being picked up and held, by having his clothes and diaper changed, and in bath time and feeding.

Activities are repeated so the child learns what to expect and develops skills. Imagine teaching a baby to blow kisses. You demonstrate it to them as you blow them kisses. Then you hold them and take their hand and cover their mouth and make the smooch noise. Then you move the hand flat to gesture how to blow air while saying "Mwah!" Songs involving hand clapping and feet tapping, patty-cake, blowing raspberries, and playing games, which all involve gentle touch. All of these are ways to insert physical affection to squirming toddlers.

As a child learns to walk, she often stumbles and falls. She seeks comfort and reassurance as she shows her mom where she scraped on her hands. Mom checks her hands and brushes her off and gives her daughter a cuddle. When the girl feels secure again, she will go play again.

As a young child exercises independence, he practices things he is learning. He may resist being held, wriggle away from hugs, refuse to sit on dad's lap or kiss grandma. Parents must find a way to squeeze affection into everyday life. Simple goodnight hugs, high-5's, and light shoulder squeezes are invaluable ways to give him needed touch. Positive touch can be playful, as in giving approving pats on the head or functional help by tying shoes or helping him put on his jacket.

Elementary School Age

It is important to not treat a child harshly. He is at an age to move quickly and does not observe everything. He may do potentially dangerous behavior as he learns. If he takes his bike and rides in the street, his parents can remain calm and teach with a firm but gentle corrective touch. They can tap his shoulder, touch his back and guide him back home. Then they can sit down and talk about how to be safe and where to ride the bike and end with a hug. Positive touch needs to far outweigh any restrictive contact from his parents. This reinforces the feelings of love and acceptance his father has for him.

Roughhousing is an important part of learning for school-age children. Play fighting by being rough and tumble allows children to learn think and adapt helps children deal with minor discomfort and resolve to problem-solving logical thought and burn energy in a productive way. Even though it may seem counter-intuitive, rough play reduces violence. A child who has gotten their energy and adaptive skills worked out is ready to have more focus in the classroom. (DeBenedet, 2011).

Privacy and safe boundaries are important to teach from an early age. Skin is a natural boundary because the barrier provided against potentially outside chemicals and exposure. Children can learn that the part of their body covered by swimming gear is private and not to be touched by others. There may be times when a parent is washing private areas or under special conditions a doctor for a limited time might check this part of the body. Children can learn to give parents or older siblings space to change clothes or take a bath. Children can set boundaries for themselves and should not be forced to kiss grandma or to hug strangers. Learning to say "No" to uncomfortable or unwanted touch by others is a skill that helps them as they enter their tween years.

Tweens and Teens

Preteens and teens bodies and minds are flooded with hormones and new emotions. Youth begin to differentiate from their families to put aside childish ways. Parents and trusted adults need to stay engaged to doubly-reassure the adolescent's worth in this time frame. This can be done through verbal praise, quality time, taking care of the teen's needs, and loving affection. As teens attempt to become responsible for their own life, they will inevitably make mistakes. A parent can convey love through respectful conversation ending with warm embrace. For a tween, he may be putting headphones on and continuing to play games after bedtime. His mother can come in and tap him on the leg. He may respond with surprise and denying what he is up to. His mom can signal him to take his headphones off and then talk about following these rules. She can take the temptations away and give him a hair toss on the way out to make sure things are good between them. These actions lessen the impact of negative messages teens may feel about peer- acceptance and fluctuating self-worth.

Parents and other adults can be aware of teens changing bodies and their feelings about development. Parents can adjust touch to continue to be respectful and non-sexually obtrusive. If a dad is teaching a teen to drive, they can demonstrate how to correctly position the mirrors and hands on the steering wheel, by guiding the hands and grip to the right place. The dad can be respectful to not do any sudden moves to interfere unless it is a safety issue. He can offer reassuring touch and feedback when the car is parked again. The family culture of affection from pre-birth will continue to affirm and display love and acceptance to teens.

We can modify how the child was treated to be more age-appropriate for a teen by giving pats on the back instead of pats on the head. An intense bear hug can adjust to a side-hug, back hug, (where the parent gives a hug from behind), or try brugs (bro's giving strong handclasps, chest bumps and pats on the backside). Staying connected through touch such as high 5's, squeezes on the shoulder, or kisses on the cheek can help validate a teen. For more playful interactions, a parent can wrestle, give them a foot or back massage, or even sit next to them and bump legs.

Interactions with teen boys or girls may involve different strategies. Teen boys may feel it is unmanly to get hugs from his mom. He may prefer a shoulder-to-shoulder interaction. This conveys a sense of camaraderie rather than a face-to-face talk which may feel confrontational. Initiate interactions while riding together in the car with a hair tousle. Connect with your teen by taking a ride on the subway seated next to each other, giving him a fist bump, or playing sports or working on the car or gaming together. This communicates to him that he is seen and respected by his parent, while contact is a natural part of the activity.

Teen girls may prefer more face-to-face activities such as going out for a coffee, or a meal or going shopping together. Touch her on the arm while talking or touch her shoulder to admire the clothes as she models them or hold her hand when walking to the mall. Doing her hair or sharing make-up tips is a bonding experience with subtle touch included.

When parents give sufficient physical positive interaction, this can help the family to be more peaceful and cooperative. Each teen is unique and may go through stages where they allow less contact or in another phase where they desire constant reassurance.

Teens need lots of affirmation as they may feel self-doubt and their bodies change and mature. When a teen is receiving enough positive affirmative touch in the home from his parents, he will be less likely to be looking to get his affirmation and touch needs met through sexual relationships. His developing brain and emotions may be unprepared to understand the decisions he may make. Especially boys receive the message that they need to find a girlfriend or deal with near total lack of touch. Positive touch from parents and trusted adults signal acceptance and love. These messages can offset negative messages in the culture about being male. Positive non-sexual touch satisfies touch needs and eliminates the vacuum of need.

Teens who have learned how to confidently say "No" to abusive or inappropriate touch will be able to navigate through the growing pressures of sex. They must learn how drinking alcohol or doing drugs inhibits clear thinking and could expose them to abusive touch of rape, assault, date rape, same-sex rape, abusive relationships, HIV and aids and venereal diseases and pregnancy. (Pickhardt, 2012)

Enough loving touch helps inoculate people against negative, abusive, and premature sexual touch. The more positive interaction they have had with parents, family and friends the more quickly they can discern and leave abusive relationships.

Young Adults

Entering their twenties, young adults make a transition to education, jobs, and relationships. At university, a young person exercises their choice without a lot of parental input. Young adults choose who can touch their body and under what conditions. Positive touch is respecting your own body and that of others.

Having a pattern of healthy touch will continue to safeguard them from relying on unhealthy relationships for affirmation. A young adult who continues to have hugs, kisses, back rubs, and shoulder pats from parents and close friends will continue to benefit from the touch. A young woman gets touch needs met by hugging and draping an arm on the shoulder of her female and male friends. There are parties with mind-altering substances and an attitude of openness to touch. People will have to decide how they will treat themselves and follow through with good boundaries.

On the other hand, young men may be unsure of the best way to get their need for touch met other than dating. Being involved in sports clubs, church groups, theater where the community is there to positively interact helps meet needs. It is important for everybody to share hugs, friendly handshakes, and kisses on the cheek as true acceptance.

Adults

It is important to help care for those we live with. Most people understand basic needs for sleep, food and oxygen but would not include touch as a necessity. Touch feels like something set aside for those in a happy, healthy, loving relationship. Far too many people live without daily human contact. People have either infantilized touch or exaggerated it by giving long embraces and swaying with hands clasped together. In adulthood, daily affirmative touch need continues.

Because it is essential to all of us, it is important to develop touch habits. Engage others with gestures of non-sexual hugs, kisses on cheeks, pats on the back and arms, supportive touches on the shoulder.

As you go about life, slow down interactions with loved ones to truly experience the feeling of comfort. Friends can show empathy and speak words but adding a meaningful touch on the arm invokes a much deeper bonding. The love hormone is activated and bonds people together in a deep way.

Adults can make set times to sit and hold hands with others in their household. This can bring cohesiveness and helps people feel less combative towards each other. Adults can add in greetings and farewells such as a hug and a kiss to those others entering or exiting the home. Couples in long relationships have shown that hugging and kissing were the most important factors to feelings of happiness. (Indiana, 2011)

If you have missed out on having much physical interaction in your long-term relationships, it is never too late to start. Just be intentional about adding affection into the daily routine of life.

In the business arena, people can be warm towards their coworkers. They can express appreciation as they touch their colleagues' shoulder. They can make eye contact and intentionally give a reassuring pat as they hand them paperwork or a coffee.

As we interact with others in the community and you can purposefully insert touch into your everyday life. There are many people who are waiting for someone to acknowledge them and are facing a difficult struggle. A friendly touch on the arm or hand can brighten their spirits.

Especially for single adults, it is important to have friends or clubs that you are involved with where you can get regular touch. If you attend church, find a way to greet many people with hugs or handshakes. You can volunteer to help in the infant and toddler area.

Become friends with a single mom or dad and go hang out with their family to get and receive more touch. Make friends with a family and become an extra set of hands to care for little ones. If you are a man, you can organize a night out with the guys to give the husband a time with other men. If you are a woman, the kids can stay home with their dad while you have a girls' outing.

Go out and spread affection by acting in local theater, playing contact sports or getting your hair washed and styled. Buy some soft cuddly clothes or a fleece blanket. Take a long warm bath and give yourself a massage with lavender-infused coconut oil.

Elderly

Elderly people can become touch deprived as they age and become socially isolated. They may live alone or in assisted-living facilities and may not have opportunities for a normal exchange of affection. Care staff may give some touch in their daily care and transfers. Family, friends and caregivers can help older people improve joint mobility, relieve muscle pain, and give emotional support through giving a short massage. A hug or a kiss, holding an elderly person's hand expresses value and care. Frequently touching them while having a short conversation is life-giving to the elderly.

Psychologist Janice Kiecolt-Glaser believes that older people need greater amount of physical contact than younger people because it creates an improved immune system and psychological well-being. (Kale, 2016). A cranky old lady may just be in a severe hug shortage due to having to live on her own too long. Implementing hugs and massage can be a way to start creating some softening in her personality and healing touch.

Another option is to get a pet for an older individual living alone. The pet gives them someone else to care for and can get some benefits from stroking an animal.

In the whole life cycle, from pre-born infants to elderly, positive touch is needed to benefit health and personal well-being. Adults can instigate positive touch to the young and elderly by setting a standard of good interactions. Everyone needs to have comfort, acceptance and love expressed to them. The good touch benefits all of us in society by creating a more cohesive, friendly atmosphere and greater health.

Feel Good Now Activity

Volunteer to read to your friends' children.

Volunteer with special needs adults. Go visit

grandma and her friends in the retirement village

and give them pedicures or hand massages.

* * * *

DeBenedet, A. T., & Cohen, L. J. (2011). The Art of Roughhousing: Good Old-Fashioned Horseplay and Why Every Kid Needs It (English Language ed.). Quirk Books.

Kale, S. (2016, November 9). The Life of the Skin Hungry Can You Go Crazy From a Lack of Touch? https://www.vice.com/en_us/article/d3gzba/the-life-of-the-skin-hungry-can-you-go-crazy-from-a-lack-of-touch

Indiana University. (2011, July 5). Couples report gender differences in relationship, sexual satisfaction over time. Https://Newsinfo.Iu.Edu. https://newsinfo.iu.edu/news/page/normal/18996.html

Mariana M. Brosnan

McKenna, J. (2007). Cosleeping Around the World.
Https://Www.Naturalchild.Org.
https://www.naturalchild.org/articles/james_mckenna/cosleeping_world.html

Pickhardt, C. (2012, November 26). Surviving Your Child's Adolescence.
https://www.psychologytoday.com/nz/blog/surviving-your-childs-
adolescence/201211/adolescence-and-physical-affection-parents

~~~~

Chapter 11: Support other's recovery

Patricia had grown up with an emotionally and physically abusive father and married a man with a similar temperament. Even though she had ended the marriage, she had never healed from the experience. Her daughter Alicia came to visit and greeted her mother with a warm hug. Patricia stiffened and then told her daughter how disappointed she was that she had been not visited sooner. Alicia felt rejected and hurt but realized this was her mother's unhealed heart talking. She hoped one day her mom would be healed and be able to accept her love.

Boundaries

Skin is the physical boundary to help delineates where one person ends, and another begins. People have spiritual, emotional, sexual, time and resource boundaries. A person with healthy boundaries is like a country that knows where its borders begin and end, respects the sovereignty of other nations and resists encroachment from others.

In some cultures, the individual boundary is less important than the group boundary. The needs of the group for closeness may outweigh individuals needs for personal space. The individual may adapt to close quarters when they are riding in a small car with a lot of people. In other times in meetings, elders in the Yup'ik tribe, like many cultures, will have a place of honor and other people sit in a less valued place.

When someone has good boundaries, she has firm spatial identity while remaining flexible if the boundary needs to adjust. A healthy person respects personal space but can accommodate crowding on a city bus without feeling violated or disrespected.

A person with little or no boundaries does not know where she begins and ends and likewise where others outside herself begin and end. This may play out by poking their nose into other's business or sharing all their business with everyone. These people may be heard saying, "I'm an open book." or "I'm just trying to help."

Another type of boundary is extremely rigid. A person may react to previous disrespect from others who ignored and jumped their boundaries. They may set unmovable, impenetrable walls. Even in the face of sound logic or overwhelming evidence she cannot reset her boundary to a healthy place. An example is when a woman is dumped by her boyfriend, she may decide to never trust another guy again. Even if she meets a kind-hearted person she sticks with her original decision.

A person with an enmeshed boundary feels no right to dictate other's behavior towards them. They go along with whatever has been told to them and may not have an idea of their own ideas about life or their own body. Their boundary is unclear and permeable so that they are unable to differentiate their own self from others.

Some people may appear to have healthy boundaries but then when a small bit of pressure is applied, the boundary collapses. This is the person who says they will go out for just one drink and ends up drinking way too much. They attempt to set a boundary, but family or friends sneak around or push until it falls without much resistance. There may be healthy boundaries in some areas of their life and none in other parts of their life.

A person who is afflicted with skin hunger or past abuse may be exhibiting extreme rigidity or may have collapsible boundaries. They have learned that they are not allowed to set good boundaries or that the lines they set will be disrespected. Someone who grew up with unhealthy boundary-hoppers has not learned how to respectfully honor themselves. They might have no idea what the healthy boundary should be.

Recognize skin hunger signs

Unstable boundaries are a clue that there may have been past abuse or neglect. Other signs may be avoiding touch or cowering when you attempt to hug him. He may be overly touchy or tend to sexualize every touch. Observe him and request permission to hug or pat his shoulder. Try to recognize what in him is broken without judging or pitying him. (Domesticshelter, 2015)

She may excel in some areas of her life but in other ways, she is immature or naïve. She may view life in an extremely distorted way. She may be overstressed and overreact to stressful situations.

Inform yourself by finding local or online resources. Be prepared to let the person lead the recovery as you play supporting role. Know that it might be in phases. The person may not be aware of how past trauma is affecting their current life. They may not believe that their life can change.

It is helpful to remember that when a person has suffered abuse or trauma, frequent, repeated acts of kindness to them will alter their view of the world. It can change from a frightening, hostile, chaotic victim approach to choose a more positive outcome for their life.

"To touch is to give life." (Michelangelo)

The steps are a similar process to what your own self-diagnosis in Chapter 9.

Access their readiness

Talk to her and gauge her openness to address what has gone on in her life.
Ask her what does she feel is the most overwhelming thing?
What is the thing that needs to be addressed first?

She may be aware of the initial event that started her down this road. If you together can find the root of the behavior and unravel it, symptoms will disappear.

As you talk with her, see if she has the desire and motivation to change. It will be up to her to drive the process and your role is as a support person. When she seems ready to start, talk about what you feel the steps to healing and a better life will be.

As you proceed, she may need the help of a professional or trained assistance. Be patient. Getting well is hard work and she will need time.

Spiritually Ready

Some questions to ask may be: Did you have a good response towards God?

Did something happen to make you doubt God or lose your faith?

What is your perception of God?

Do you believe that there is a creator who made you with a purpose?

What is your purpose?

How does that play out in your life?

What would you like your spiritual life look like?

Emotionally Ready

Do you feel secure and happy now?

Did something happen in the past that changed that?

Did you feel emotionally wanted and cared for by both your parents?

Were there any incidents that you felt insecure or worried?

Were you abused emotionally?

Did you feel nurtured and protected emotionally?

Did you feel safe to explore the world and meet new people?

Do you feel emotionally stable?

Do you struggle with low self-esteem, depression, busyness, or a lack of ability accomplish things?

What would emotional stability look like to you?

Physically Ready

Did you have your touch needs met?

Were you physically or sexually abused?

Did your parents neglect you?

Did an authority figure physically take advantage of you?

Did another person do things physically to you that you did not like?

Did someone touch you in a way that viscerally felt bad or off in some way?

Did someone take rather than give positive touch?

What would normal interaction look like to you?

Mentally Ready

Do you feel you were raised by mentally stable parents?

Do you feel you have stable mental health?

Do you suffer from either extreme lows or highs?

Do you take things too personally?

Do you suddenly cut off relationships with people you perceive hurt you?

Do you know your own core values?

Do you feel able to keep your values in the face of other people's opposing values?

Are you open to changing your views when information is presented?

What would mental stability be for you in your life?

Prepare to walk with them as they progress

When someone takes on the process of healing, there may be giant leaps, small steps or possible regression. The mind and soul begin to heal, and then new habits can be established. Healing comes and the practical side adjusting to the new mindset must be practiced. The process could be quick or could roll out over her lifetime.

Engage as a support person

What are different touch types she enjoys that are non-sexual that you can provide? As the support person, you can keep safe touch as she guides what touch she might like. Maintain your own comfort zone of touch. Ask her to give feedback on what type of touch helps or distracts.

When he seems to be feeling sad, offer words of support and ask whether you can hug or touch his shoulder. Later, ask for feedback if the touch was welcome, annoying, soothing, or just condescending or dismissive. Help him to know himself better and for you to communicate the touch you enjoy also.

"Let us touch the dying, the poor, the lonely

and the unwanted according to the graces we

have received and let us not be ashamed or

slow to do the humble work."

Mother Teresa of Calcutta

Setbacks

People may have minefields, words that have explosive meanings to them. It may be like potholes, circular ideas they get stuck in and keep rehashing. Approach them gently and respectfully with a small bit of information. Is their response positive to the possibility of future change? If they can make small gains at first, this success can give them motivation to continue.

To help someone, you must have learned the lessons yourself. If you have taken the steps to healing and freedom and successfully practiced them, you may be stable enough to help another person.

If you are still working on your own balance, help connect the injured person to someone who can help. If you have struggled with the same issues yourself, then you can practice alongside them until you have mastered the skills and can become a mentor.

Support your friend by respecting their boundaries and giving them affection. Protect touch with them and make sure it is safe, non-sexual, and without demands to be reciprocated. Be a good example of healthy living.

If they refuse help, they may feel so damaged that nothing can make it better. In this case, pray for them for their best life, and speak healing, hopeful words to them. Do not give up! They may have given up temporarily, but you can keep putting the possibility of a good future in front of them. If they someday feel, they want to change, you may be one they reach for help.

Professional help

Engage professional support as needed. If you feel out of your depth knowledge, then it may be time to help find resources. If your friend has suffered deep wounds, a trained counselor may be needed. A list is provided in Therapy for Extreme Skin Hunger chapter of professional help. Ask the professional, how to support the process.

Your role is as a coach or cheerleader for your friend. You can see the negative impact that lack of good touch has done. You cannot do the steps for them, but you can offer support. The person must do the work. If you are working harder than the person in recovery, you are working too hard. Help them by being an example or referring them to a professional.

Feel Good Now Activity

Find your boundaries of personal space with different family members and friends. Blindfold yourself and have them slowly approach you while talking. Then have them stop when you react. The person can then reach out and touch your hand or shoulder and keep talking. See how you respond to personal space and boundaries.

* * * *

domesticshelters.org. (2015, August 12). Hugs that Don't Trigger Fear in Survivors. Domesticshelters https://www.domesticshelters.org/domestic-violence-articles-information/hugs-that-don-t-trigger-fear-in-survivors

Chapter 12: Community Resources

Japanese are busier than ever and lonelier as it has become the norm to live alone. To combat feeling blue, an anti-loneliness chair is being marketed to older people. The chair is dressed like a tall fabric doll with long arms so that a person can sit on the lap and get a hug. The chair is designed to promote a tranquil feeling.

(Im, 2017)

Loneliness has infiltrated the spaces in lives where community has retreated. Where natural networks had been in place with extended families living together, now more people than ever are living alone. Sweden has the highest rate with 47 percent of its population living solo. In Great Britain it is nearly 1 in 3. People are choosing and able to live alone because of the welfare system that financially supports living alone. By contrast the Japanese have 6 million elderly who are living alone and feeling the loneliness acutely. The Japanese are looking to technology or paying for human company to help people connect. (Brannan, A. 2019)

Some of these ideas are to rent a friend to take to dinner or an activity as a companion. If you want to eat with a less chatty friend, the Moomin house cafe has large stuffed animals to sit at the table with you. Cat cafes are everywhere so you can relax while stroking the cute creatures. The more exotic might try the bunny café where they can have some coffee and watch a bunny hop around. (Wright, 2020)

You can meet new friends by going to a bar in the Golden Gai area. Only five people are allowed in each mini bar to make it easy to mingle. The host or hostess bar has cute men and women to talk with as you have a drink. Some who live alone make a stop at the cuddle café where they can have a woman give them hugs before they head home. (JP, 2019) All of these are to simulate normal human interaction.

Self-help style groups

Cuddle Therapy is a new field where trained professionals meet touch needs through non-sexual cuddling. At the first appointment the staff and client set boundaries for acceptable touch. Both are wearing comfortable clothes while a variety of touch is exchanged from hair being stroked, holding hands, back rubs, spooning, and talking while one's face is held.

Professional cuddler Samantha Hess wrote how cuddling benefits people in her book Touch: The Power of Human Connection. She opened her Portland, Oregon cuddling business in 2014 and received more than 10,000 emails a week for people wanting to connect.

David Wheitner, a psychologist and life coach authored Snuggle Party. This guide helps people looking to create a cuddle group to get some valuable affection. (Wheitner et. all, 2014) He gives suggestions for guidelines to keep touch safe and enjoyable and therapeutic.

Informal groups who gather to get more touch have sprung up. Cuddle parties are posted on social media to advertise a meeting. The dress attire is pajamas or comfortable clothes. As people arrive and mingle, they find partners to talk to and cuddle with. Partners will sit holding hands, spoon or hug each other. It is a way to get comfort and stress-reduced, to get a hug and have warm bodily contact. (Fortenbury, 2014)

Another way of doing touch with a friend is through contact yoga. This involves two people doing yoga, while their bodies remain in contact with each other. It gives a non-stop effect of skin-to-skin feeling. It can be very calming and nurturing.

If you cannot find a friend to do yoga, try goat yoga. You are doing your pose and while a baby goat climbs to the highest stable point of your body.

Besides yoga there is dance. Contact Improv is a style of dance where there is constant contact. People slide and roll their bodies against their partner in a constant fluid motion. The partners lean into each other, creating times of balance and counterbalance movement.

Another option is to have a furry friend and cuddle buddy. You can foster or adopt a dog or cat. This is beneficial as you have a live animal with a personality to relate to and offers a lowering of stress by stroking a pet.

If your apartment does not allow pets, get a couple of Pari a brainchild of the Japanese. This furry stuffed animal and his pair are for friends or couples. When you hug one Pari, the other one vibrates to receive the hug and let you know your friend is thinking of you. (Belz, 2017)

Getting a soft stuffed toy or heavy blanket can be a comfort. Soft animals give you something to hold and cuddle. Gravity blankets are weighted blankets that help people deal with lack of human touch and restless feeling when going to bed. By giving an amount of pressure people report feeling grounded and calm when using the blankets.

Ken Nwadike Jr wanted to run the Boston Marathon the year after the bombing. He missed qualifying by a mere 23 seconds and decided to video himself giving free hugs. He decided to keep up the project as a peace activist and to give out hugs at races and social justice events. He has been involved in de-escalating the riots following the death of George Floyd, a black man in the U.S. in 2020. (Nwadike, n.d.)

Giving out free hugs mean you get and give them at the same time. This in-person touch delivers soothing psychological benefits. Getting a massage can be a rewarding way to get some physical comfort.

When I was going through a particularly, stressful time in my life, I would schedule a massage about every three weeks. On a bad day, I would count how many more days until my next massage. Just knowing that I had a massage scheduled, helped me get through the day. Thirty-minute massages were too short and one-and-a-half hour ones felt like torture to me. An hour was enough time to relax without my brain starting to think up a million other productive things I could be doing with this time.

I did not enjoy the hot rocks (I do not get it), the deep tissue (who needs that much pain?) and couples who take turns massage (after his massage, why does he fall asleep and I get skipped). I typically got a therapeutic massage where specific muscles that had knots were targeted and I would leave feeling relaxed and in less pain.

The strangest things to happen in a massage were in Costa Rica, when the massage therapist laid on top of me to "stretch me out" and in Taiwan, the massager lady walked on my back with her full-body weight. Although she was a smaller lady, I still felt my lungs feeling a bit crushed. I highly recommend massage to ease tension, get nice touch and reset.

Massage helps the body by increasing blood flow and this promotes the muscle tone and elasticity. By having better circulation, reduces stress and anxiety, and the experience of release of physical and emotional trauma, even the skin looks better as it becomes more smooth and supple. A rub of the abdomen can improve digestion and relieve gas and bowel distress. Psychologically massage leaves you feeling reconnected with your body emotionally and physically, helps you forget about your worries and helps you become relaxed even to the point of dozing off. Massage is great because you can schedule it and anticipate the payoff. (Evastar, 2010)

Couples who give each other frequent touch benefit from this touch by having their mood modulated and creating more intense bonds of psychological intimacy. In one study, happy couples touched each other 85 percent of the times they were in the same physical space. (PBS Connections, 2013) This close relationship-based affection has a more intense cumulative effect than touch between strangers. The short-term gains are a feeling of support and psychological well-being. Long-term the affection solidified and maintained the couples' intimate feelings towards each other. The better their relationship was the more touch benefited them.

As humans we were made for touch and intimacy. When we are without friends or family around to give us the affection we need, getting a dog or fluffy blanket can help offset our needs for touch. Massage can help to get the benefits of touch. The fact remains that the best touch we can get for long-term benefits is in a partner relationship or in family where daily gifts of touch warm each other.

Feel Good Now Activity

Have a cuddle party solo or with friends.

Everyone wears flannel pajamas or comfortable

clothing. Wrap a soft blanket around you and

have a talk or just chill and watch a movie.

* * * *

Belz, K. (2017, April 10). This stuffed animal gives hugs, and we need one ASAP. Https://Hellogiggles.Com/. https://hellogiggles.com/lifestyle/technology/this-stuffed-animal-gives-hugs

Brannan, A. (2019, September 4). Top 10 Loneliest Countries in the World. Immigroup. https://www.immigroup.com/news/top-10-loneliest-countries-world#:~:text=%231%20%2D%20Sweden&text=Sweden%20tops%20the%20list%20when,loneliest%20countries%20in%20the%20world

Evastar. (2010, May 10). The Physical and Physiological Effects of Massage [Online Forum Post]. Digitalworldz. https://www.digitalworldz.co.uk/threads/the-physical-and-physiological-effects-of-massage.236311/

Fortenbury, J. (2014, July 15). Fighting Loneliness with Cuddle Parties. Theatlantic http://www.theatlantic.com/health/archive/2014/07/fighting-loneliness-with-cuddle-parties/373335/

Hess, S. (2015). Touch: The Power of Human Connection (2nd ed.). Fulcrum Solutions LLC.

Im, J. (2017, November 7). 8 of Japan's craziest, anti-loneliness attractions. Https://Nypost.Com. https://nypost.com/2014/11/07/8-of-japans-craziest-anti-lonellness-attractions/

Nwadike, K. (n.d.). About Free Hugs Campaign Free Hugs Project. Https://Freehugsproject.Com/. Retrieved July 1, 2017, from https://freehugsproject.com/about-free-hugs-campaign/

PBS Connections. (2013, November 26). https://spsptalks.wordpress.com/2013/11/26/touch-as-an-interpersonal-emotion-regulation-process-in-couples-daily-lives-the-mediating-role-of-psychological-intimacy/. Https://Spsptalks.Wordpress.Com/. https://spsptalks.wordpress.com/2013/11/26/touch-as-an-interpersonal-emotion-regulation-process-in-couples-daily-lives-the-mediating-role-of-psychological-intimacy/

Want to sleep with a good looking guy or a pretty girl? Then Check out Japan's Cuddle Cafes! (2019, April 10). Https://Jpninfo.Com/. https://jpninfo.com/53515

Wheitner, D., Reynolds, K., Davis, J., & Baker, A. (2014). The Snuggle Party Guidebook: Create Deeper Friendships, Decrease Loneliness, & Enjoy Nurturing Touch Community (1st ed.). Divergent Drummer Publications.

Wright, J. (2020, April 17). What Happens When We Can't Touch Each Other? Skin Hunger.Refinery29. https://www.refinery29.com/en-us/2020/04/9694663/what-is-skin-hunger-people-touching-contact

Chapter 13: Extreme Skin Hunger

In 1800, a feral boy was found in the woods in France. It is believed that parental neglect drove him to flee his home. Psychiatrist Phillipe Pinel evaluated him and believed the boy was an idiot. Doctor Jean Marc Gaspard Itard took the boy home and named him Victor. Itard educated the boy and documented his progress. Over time he could understand rudimentary language but never spoke. During the five years, Itard determined Victor was severely mentally delayed due to lack of human touch and interaction. (Victor of Aveyron. (n.d.)

Parents should be the first and most important source of affirming touch to their children. Unfortunately, one or both parents are involved in over 91 percent of cases of abuse and neglect. (American Society for the Positive Care of Children, 2018) Substance abuse or mental illness in parents increased even the chances of maltreatment in their young.

In the U.S. in 2018, there were 678,000 children neglected or abused. (U.S. Department of Health & Human Services Administration for Children and Families., 2019) Neglect is when basic needs are not provided such as clean food, water, basic care, shelter and supervision. Physical abuse includes hitting, slapping, kicking, punching and shaking him. Emotional abuse is denying a child the basic physical interactions of hugging, kissing, affection, and instead calling her mean names, shaming her or exposing her to violence in the home.

A baby starts at a disadvantage if she is conceived in a hostile, or unstable relationship or parents with substance abuse or mental illness problems. Infants under one year are the most neglected age group. At this crucial stage, the neglect causes developmental delays, emotional insecurity, lack of nutrition, less human touch and mental stimulation. Not having basic needs met predisposes him to lifelong tendency for failure in his life. (Why Marriage Matters, n.d.)

The more neglect and abuse that a child has suffered, the less she is able to maintain her own health, her own sense of well-being, her own ability to succeed in relationships. She will start to believe the world is an unsafe place that she should avoid and be less willing to try new things or meet new people. (Good Therapy, 2019)

In cases of mistreatment or physical abuse by their parents, it is important to understand that children prefer negative attention to apathy. (Hill, 2015) A child cannot survive without attachment to her parents. Being mistreated is interpreted as warped caring and the experience of this kind of treatment develops mental impairments around relationships. For children of drug-abusing parents they often develop an ambivalent attachment where they refuse to invest in any decisions or an anxious attachment. They believe that the people they hope in, will disappear without any warning. Children who are physically abused would likely have an avoidant attachment style to not engage any type of relationship building. Any person who reaches out to them would have a long road to establish a level of trust to build a relationship.

Children can have PTSD when they grow up in a household where the parents relationship has domestic violence. By having to be on guard for a violent episode, they become hyper-vigilant where their brain is rewired to look for threatening faces and be on high alert to sense for danger. A male child can learn from his abusive father to dominate through physical force. A female child may learn manipulation and by using emotions to control others to try to survive. These children can suffer from low self-esteem and low connection to their relatives.

A father may be absent due to neglect, divorce, having separated from his family, illness, overwork, or extended times away where the father cannot have regular access to his children due to things like military service. This prolonged void may communicate rejection and disinterest to their children.

More than 1 in 4 children grow up without a father in the home. (all4kids, 2018) By not having a father present in their home to offer love and attention, children are more apt to experience unplanned pregnancies, depression, suicide-attempts, and lack of success academically or socially. Absent-father's homes create higher levels of psychological problems and depression for young women. Without the father present, the family is more likely to fall into poverty, increase risk for teens to become homeless and less successful future relationships.

Without a father, children are more apt to have more gender dysphoria. (Mascaro et al, 2017) Fathers' interactions reinforce a child's gender. Fathers are more rough-and-tumble with sons and talk about their strength. A daughter would be treated in a gentle way and include talk of emotions and how beautiful she is. The father's physical exchanges with his children give them cues as how to respond and helps affirm them as a boy or girl. (Yogman & Garfield, 2016)

Growing up in Alaska, in my family, the daughters and son joined in activities like sports fishing, hunting, shoveling snow from the driveway, and commercial fishing. My dad taught me how to do basic maintenance on my car including checking the oil, water and tire pressure along with changing a flat tire before I could drive my car. His influence has made us, his children know that we are resourceful and competent.

"If the power of loving touch is astounding,

the power of invasive touch is horrific."

(David Brooks)

Teen girls who have been exposed to abuse have not seen normal physical boundaries and interaction with a man. She will seek out the same type of abusive relationships. Abused teens have higher chances of engaging in risky sexual encounters and are 25 percent more likely to get pregnant. By this age they have learned that their own behavior has little effect on what comes their way and that adults cannot be trusted, and things will always be unfair for them. (O'Donnell, Quarshi, 2019)

Children who mothers are absent or not in the home suffer as they lose the person who will love them unconditionally and nurture them. Children can have poor opinions and undervalue themselves. Middle school children may demonstrate their feelings by having behavioral problems and low self-esteem. Teens can be affected by not having appropriate social skills and interpersonal strengths. (You are mom, 2018)

Inside the Iron Curtain, Romanian dictator Nicolae Ceausescu had a plan to increase industry by growing his country's population. He mandated that all women give birth to five children and outlawed birth control. He created orphanages and brainwashed the public to relinquish children to the state to be raised under the best conditions. When families had too many other children or lacked financial resources to support their young, they were abandoned or relinquished to the state. As a result, over 500,000 children were placed into state care.

The low ratio of caregivers to children made it impossible to give children enough attention and proper care. Routinely children spent all day in their beds. Many checked out mentally and would resort to banging their heads against their cribs. These orphans suffered developmental, physical, and emotional delays. Many have never recovered from the brain damage caused by severe neglect.

Brain imaging studies on the Romanian orphans who had been institutionalized showed smaller regions of the hippocampus, which regulates memory and emotions. Years later as adults, some survivors committed violent physical and sexual acts to themselves and others. These orphans had suffered being left alone for much of their childhood in overcrowded conditions and with inadequate affection, limiting their ability to have empathy towards others. (Steavenson, 2014)

Adults who were neglected as children have a difficult time giving steady care to their own children. Approximately one in three who are abused and raised in a dysfunctional family will grow up to abuse their own children. (Boyles, 2003) This generational problem repeats unless there is intervention and a change of mind and behavior. Unloving parents who have denied their child love and care, damage his self-esteem and leave him feeling insecure and unsafe. Single mothers coming out of abusive situations, can be overwhelmed, frustrated, depressed and potentially escalate with neglect or abuse towards their children.

The lingering negative effects of a lifetime of touch deficiency can lead to immaturity, speech disorders and learning or eating disorders. It can erode views of self, with feelings of worthlessness, guilt and shame, and can also cause an increase in self-harming, drug or alcohol abuse and physical malaise such as ulcers, headaches and stomach aches. (Office for National Statistics, 2017)

One study has shown that eighty percent of young adults who had at least one psychological disorder had suffered child abuse. Thirty percent of parents who abuse their own children had experience abuse as children themselves. (Boyles, 2003)

A survey of 571 individuals in the U.S. on intimate partner violence showed that 50% of men and 50% of women have experienced violence with their current partner. Domestic violence is a violation of personal boundaries and bruises the psyche. (Mental Health, 2020)

Elder abuse often happens when a spouse, adult child or caretakers become frustrated in caring for the older person and strike them. As adults age and lose their independence, they may have less mobility and have incontinent issues and loss the ability to clearly process thoughts. It can be a bit like regression to childhood. People with memory diseases like dementia or Alzheimer's can exhibit aggressive behavior can be uncooperative and violent to a caregiver. A poor response from an often overworked and overburdened helper can cause physical injury and mental distress to the elderly person.

Often an elderly or disabled person does not have a clear way to communicate to others to get help for abuse that is occurring. They may fear that they will be treated worse or not be taken care of at all.

Neglect and abuse to the young and old has devastating effects on physical development and psychological balance. Often the ones suffering the abuse feel unable to get out of the situation. Long-term loss of affection can cause brain damage and irreversible stunted growth. If this has happened to you or someone you know there is hope. Today can be a start of a new healing path for you. In the next chapter, we discuss different steps to finding freedom from these old wounds.

Feel Good Now Activity

Get some nice smelling body oil and give

yourself a full-body massage, your feet have

been waiting for this. Do not forget to include

your abdomen, back and buttocks. Massage in

the bathtub to stay extra warm.

* * * *

all4kids. (2018, June 7). A Father's Impact on Child Development. Https://Www.All4kids.Org. https://www.all4kids.org/news/blog/a-fathers-impact-on-child-development/

American Society for the Positive Care of Children. (2018). Child Abuse Statistics. Https://Americanspcc.Org/. https://americanspcc.org/child-abuse-statistics/

Boyles, S. (2003, February 6). Do Sexually Abused Kids Become Abusers? Https://Www.Webmd.Com/. https://www.webmd.com/mental-health/news/20030206/do-sexually-abused-kids-become-abusers#1/

Good Therapy. (2019, November 15). Neglect. Https://Www.Goodtherapy.Org. https://www.goodtherapy.org/learn-about-therapy/issues/neglect#:~:text=Neglect%2C%20also%20referred%20to%20as,person%20they%20provide%20care%20for.&text=People%20who%20have%20been%20through,isolation%2C%20anxiety%2C%20and%20depression

Hill, T. (2015, September 9). 9 Signs of Traumatic Bonding: "Bonded to the abuser. Https://Blogs.Psychcentral.Com/. https://blogs.psychcentral.com/caregivers/2015/09/9-signs-of-traumatic-bonding-bonded-to-the-abuser/

O'Donnell, J., & Quarshi, M. (2019, January 29). The startling toll on children who witness domestic violence is just now being understood. Https://Www.Usatoday.Com/. https://www.usatoday.com/story/news/health/2019/01/29/domestic-violence-research-children-abuse-mental-health-learning-aces/2227218002/

Office for National Statistics. (2017, September 27). Impact of child abuse on later life, Crime Survey for England and Wales, year ending March 2016. Https://Www.Ons.Gov.Uk/. https://www.ons.gov.uk/peoplepopulationandcommunity/crimeandjustice/adho

cs/007527impactofchildabuseonlaterlifecrimesurveyforenglandandwalesyeare
ndingmarch2016

Mascaro, J. S., Rentscher, K. E., Hackett, P. D., Mehl, M. R., & Rilling, J. K. (2017). Child gender influences paternal behavior, language, and brain function. Behavioral neuroscience, 131(3), 262–273. https://doi.org/10.1037/bne0000199

Mental Health. (2020). Physically and Emotionally Abusive Relationships. Https://Www.Mentalhelp.Net/. https://www.mentalhelp.net/aware/physically-and-emotionally-abusive-relationships/

Steavenson, W. (2014, December 10). Ceausescu's Children. Https://Www.Theguardian.Com/. https://www.theguardian.com/news/2014/dec/10/-sp-ceausescus-children

U.S. Department of Health & Human Services Administration for Children and Families. (2019). Child Maltreatment 2018. Department of Health and Human Services. https://www.acf.hhs.gov/sites/default/files/cb/cm2018.pdf

Victor of Aveyron. (n.d.). In Wikipedia. Retrieved March 13, 2019 from https://en.wikipedia.org/wiki/Victor_of_Aveyron

Why Marriage Matters 26 Conclusions from the Social Sciences. (n.d.). Www.Familyscholars.Com. Retrieved July 12, 2019, from https://cdn.shopify.com/s/files/1/0275/9135/files/Why-Marriage-Matters.pdf?3573788516863415290

Yogman, M., & Garfield, C. (2016, July). Fathers' Roles in the Care and Development of Their Children: The Role of Pediatricians (No. 27296867). American Academy of Pediatrics. https://doi.org/10.1542/peds.2016-1128

You are mom. (2018, February 25). How an Absent Mother Affects Children. https://youaremom.com/children/absent-mother-affects-children/

Chapter 14: Therapy For Neglect Or Abuse

My Canadian friend Frank is a traveling missionary in Asia. Recently he was in Cambodia. He went for a walk in the evening browsing souvenirs. Some prostitutes asked if he was looking for company. When he said no, a couple of the women tried to drag him inside. He laughed and said, "I thought kidnapping was illegal in Cambodia." He then started talking to them about their lives.

He asked them if they had broken hearts. He explained it meant that if someone who they had counted on had severely disappointed them. One young woman said yes, and he asked if he could pray for her. He gently placed his hand on her shoulder and prayed for her heart to be healed. She began to weep as he prayed, and she immediately started feeling better. She went and brought three other friends she worked with to be prayed for. The women stated that they had broken relationships in their home with their parents and heartbreak from ex-boyfriends. Frank helps the ladies experienced healing which can start a chain reaction for their lives to change. He believes that as these women experience their hearts being whole, they will search for different work and look for positive relationships. (January 12, 2020, Personal interview, phone interview) Research supports his experience. People who have received healing prayer show the benefit is still positive after a year. (Bolens et al, 2012)

The previous chapter had some examples of neglect and abuse and the damaging effects it has on people. It is time to seek help when you recognize behaviors and attitudes that harm you and your relationships and have stopped helping you survive the pain of life.

Author and psychologist Henry Cloud states, "We change our behavior when the pain of staying the same becomes greater than the pain of changing. (Negative) consequences give us the pain that motivates us to change." (Cloud & Townsend, 2017)

In Chapter 9, where we discussed the steps to get ready to change and have more touch in your life, we briefly touched on forgiveness. The key to getting free of the past is forgiveness. This is the place to discharge the bitter memories and pain and make space for good memories and pleasurable experiences with others.

One tool that can be helpful in this process is a personal history inventory. Here you make a list of behavior that was done to you and of things that should have been done for you but were not. You also list any judgments that you made against parents, siblings or others who hurt you. Even though it is unpleasant and being numb may feel better, pain exists to indicate a wrong has been committed, so that as much as possible it can be made right.

Sara Mae wrote A Complicated Heart about the difficult relationship with her mother. She grew up with a neglectful alcoholic mother. Even as an adult, it was difficult for her to try to have a relationship and she would take month-long breaks to try to regain her own balance. She writes about going through the process of forgiving her mother, despite her mother's behavior and attitudes towards her remaining unchanged. She talks about grieving the loss of a mother that she wanted but never had. She had to discover the things she identified as loss and pain and then she could move towards forgiveness. There are two parts of forgiveness are making the decision of the mental process of going through the steps to choose to forgive and the emotional forgiveness, which releases the person from owing you. (Puder, 2019) The goal is not to reengage in a relationship with the one who hurt you but to be free of the burden of wanting revenge or payment for your pain. When you forgive, the pain dissipates.

"Unforgiveness is like drinking poison yourself

and waiting for the other person to die."

Marianne Williamson

It is a separate issue of whether or how to move into a relationship with a person who cannot or will not change abusive behavior. The person may still have the same addiction or patterns of behavior and are unable to see beyond their own pain to take responsibility for the pain they have or are causing. By being willing to forgive your parent or another person who has hurt you, you free yourself to not repeat their mistakes. You free yourself to have improved, good experiences.

Healing prayer with trained faith-based counselor or trusted friend

Find a well-respected faith-based counselor or a close friend with some training in helping people get free of their past hurts. Ask what type of training and experience they have and what type of success they have had. Find out what type of assessments will be used before or after the meetings to help you process the counseling. Each person will have a different process and it will involve some of these steps.

Read and discuss your personal history inventory with your counselor. Because the body retains and stores positive and negative experiences, you may have a physical response when you think of people who have traumatized you.

Pray to forgive those who have offended you. Repent and pray for God to forgive your response to them if you judged them. Ask God to remove all the negative effects and hurtful memories chemically stored in your cells and in the person, who hurt you.

Take one situation at a time and work through the list starting with the most important or from your earliest memories. As you begin to release them from owing you anything, the chains tying you to them will loosen and you will be free. You can begin a new way of living that you have never experienced before.

It is important to affirm that you have chosen to forgive and even if the old pain dredges itself back up, you will need to remind yourself that you have forgiven and are not interested in picking back up and reminiscing on this event.

Therapists

It is important to understand that when working with a therapist, the patient needs to be in control of any physical contact. A written document of each appointment records touch. This is based on what the client desires and reflects appropriate and agreeable with the therapist. Touch in a safe environment can rebuild trust and bring healing.

Psychotherapist Mic Hunter and social worker Jim Struve co-authored The Ethical Use of Touch in Psychotherapy (And Political Culture, 1998). They believe that therapist can support a patient through emotional support and nurturing touch in the counseling sessions. Professional help can provide a mature, stable person to help practice and establish patterns of positive physical touch.

There are many different approaches in therapy. One of those is cognitive-behavioral therapy which identifies your faulty thought patterns. Some destructive circuits included are black and white thinking, minimizing, or catastrophizing and personalization of behavior. The therapist will help you detect unhelpful cycles and critically analyze their effectiveness. You will be given new techniques to help you gain a different perspective on life.

When a child has been raised in a dysfunctional family, they need a pattern of kindness and good interactions to help them come new cycles. The longer that the child suffered, the more ingrained it will be in their psyche. The key is to never give up.

In body psychotherapy, an approach of listening and analyzing the body is used to release inner pain and emotion. The practitioner asks the patient to relax and then to identify different stress or negative feelings in the body. A patient may sense a knot in the pit of the stomach or carrying negative emotions in the shoulders. The practitioner then uses reassuring touch and leads the patient to let go of emotions, memories stored in the body. By releasing the stored memory energy, the patient can rebalance the good function and feel of a healthy body. (Good Therapy, 2018)

Regression therapy goes back to the beginning steps of touch. "Childhood comes First" is a program that recreates how positive touch would have occurred in the best circumstances. The therapist and patient establish non-touch areas of the body and guidelines for how touch will occur and progress. They build trust in a secure, safe way of increasing touch interaction. This can start with the client learning the type of non-sexual touch her own body enjoys. She can explore touch further with the feel of soft blankets, stuffed animals, and pets before moving into touching other humans. The therapist's role is to create a safe environment. The patient directs and controls the touch. The patient then learns to have control of their own body. They learn to communicate their needs and want to have affection from others. (Helfer, 1984)

Hunter and Strove observed that "healing is unlikely to occur if a positive approach to touch remains as an idea or just an intellectual concept, but it isn't actually played out, and it isn't actually changed and defined and used and build back up to what it needs to be." (Hunter & Strove, 1998)

No matter what situation of abuse or neglect you have survived it is possible to be an overcomer and be free of it. Identifying the incidents and perpetrators is helpful to unravel the pain. Working with a trusted counselor or therapist can offer invaluable support to help you achieve freedom. Practicing a positive approach to touch can be a vital part of this healing process since all aspects of us – mind, body and spirit – play a role in our healing.

Feel Good Now Activity

Volunteer at the local pet shelter to exercise and pet dogs and cats. Visit a cat café and stroke these fluffy creatures. Get a soft cuddly toy for a cuddle buddy.

* * * *

Boelens, Peter & Reeves, Roy & Replogle, William & Koenig, Harold. (2012). The Effect of Prayer on Depression and Anxiety: Maintenance of Positive Influence One Year After Prayer Intervention. International journal of psychiatry in medicine. 43. 85-98. 10.2190/PM.43.1.f.

Good Therapy. (2018, May 16). Body Psychotherapy. Https://Www.Goodtherapy.Org/. http://www.goodtherapy.org/body-psychotherapy.html

Hanks, F. (2015). When Your Body Is Not Your Own. Http://Www.Emptyhospitals.Org/. http://www.emptyhospitals.org/when-your-body-is-not-your-own/

Helfer, R. (1984). Childhood Comes First: A Crash Course in Childhood for Adults (2nd ed.). C Henry Kempe.

Hunter, M. G., & Struve, J. (1998). The Ethical Use of Touch in Psychotherapy (And Political Culture). SAGE Publications, Inc.

Mae, S. (2019). The Complicated Heart: Loving Even When It Hurts. B&H Books.

Puder, D. (2019, April 11). The Science Behind Forgiveness and How it Affects Our Mental Health. https://www.psychiatrypodcast.com/psychiatry-psychotherapy-podcast/2019/4/10/what-is-forgiveness

~~~~

Mariana M. Brosnan

Chapter 15: Hope For A Normal Life

Children who got many doses of physical affirmation felt loved and accepted and became more happy, serene and empathic with others. They were able to deal with difficult people in a positive way, had balanced mental health and had more brotherly love. (Schwartz, 2017)

Good self-care

Steady work is needed to establish a new level of contact after coming from past touch deprivation or trauma. Good self-care is treating yourself in an honorable and caring way like you would care for a beloved loved one. Imagine your life with the amount of touch with your friends and family that you desire. Give yourself hand or foot massages to keep positive touch as well. It is time to begin and not allow yourself to slip back into old negative touch or non-contact patterns during challenging times.

Spiritual caretaking

To take care of yourself spiritually, it begins with hearing from God. He speaks to each person in individual ways. Sometimes that can be by reading the Bible, speaking and listening to God in prayer, trusting him with what you and others need or hope for, and talking with other who have the same faith. There are many characteristics of God. He is good, just and merciful. He created each person and wants to rescue us from our own selfish ways and wants to develop a father/child relationship with each of us. God promises his followers to be with them in trouble and to bless them.

By filling your spirit up on positive things, there will not be space to entertain negative ideas and you will naturally be a source of love to others. By replacing constant thoughts to beat yourself up about your past mistakes or failures, you can start to forgive yourself and speak the good things God says about you. What you speak over yourself, you will internalize and demonstrate outwardly.

Emotional soul satisfied

The needs of the soul are love and acceptance and purpose. God says he will supply every need. He has known you every day of your life. He has seen your internal and external choices and responses to the things people have done to you. He understands your motives and needs and wants to improve your life.

God accepts you right where you are. He wants to remove you from situations that are hurtful to you and others. He wants to bring peace and repair to your life.

He has a purpose for your life, in which you feel fulfilled. He created each person uniquely with a destiny and a sense of purpose. We can come to him with our needs and ask him to fill us and to change things that are harming us.

"I say this because I know what I have planned for you," says the Lord. "I have good plans for you. I do not plan to hurt you. I plan to give you hope and a good future. Jeremiah 29:11 (ICB, 2011)

Imagine the work of a potter. She uses various types of clays and shapes different forms that are heated at a range of temperatures for a specific purpose. She creates a vase to hold flowers, a pot for the kitchen and an urn for burial. The highest function is for each piece to fulfill what they were created for.

A person starts to believe he is not valuable because of the way his family or friends have undervalued him or misused him. He will need to reconnect to his designer to fulfill the expression that he was created for in order to overcome his past. This may be through software engineering, mothering, music, science or dance. Trying to live unconnected from his creator and intended purpose, is trying to assemble a puzzle without the lid of the box as a guide and with pieces removed or added from other puzzles.

As you begin to see your purpose then you can move towards emotional wellness. Mature and healthy people are part of emotional interactions and that reveal areas of needed growth. Establish boundaries over your body, your time, money and resources. Show up in the commitments that you have in your family, friends and workplace.

Eliminate or change things that disturb your peace.

Emotional intelligence, your EQ, can be expressed by deciding ahead of time on your limits and being prepared to state a gracious and firm "No." Practice setting and communicating your physical boundaries by knowing how you feel and stopping touch immediately that is untimely, inappropriate or unwanted. According to Daniel Goldman, psychologist and author of Emotional Intelligence, a good EQ is more important than IQ as a predictor of personal and professional success. (Goleman, 2005)

Honor culture

Replace negative self-talk and demeaning language with words of honor, encouragement, self-respect and value. Caring for yourself is bringing your own stability. Being out of balance, you cannot offer reliable support to others. Modeling good care for yourself is a necessary step before caring for others.

Shel Silversteen illustrates this concept in his children's book, *The missing piece meets the big O.* It demonstrates a person searching for themselves in relationships and eventually realizing that he must grow to wholeness first. The missing piece is a triangle who cannot move due to his sharp edges. He looks for a circle missing a triangle so they can roll together. He meets shapes with too many other relationships or who do not know how to have a relationship. He meets a girl who he fits well with and they roll well together until he grows out of the relationship. They cannot smoothly roll and separate. He meets a circle who is rolling along by herself. She encourages him to try rolling alone. He strains and the hard edges come off and they can roll together. For me, the book illustrates the concept of becoming well, healed and encouraging others to follow this path. People can become whole when they give up trying to fill the "missing areas" in their lives with other people, social media, attention or control and become brave enough to address their own life issues and grow. (Silverstein, 2006)

Physical

Physical self-care includes getting enough rest or downtime, sleeping well, exercising, maintaining body strength and flexibility, being purposeful in physical interaction with family and friends through an embrace or positive touch, smiling at people, and making the world a warmer place.

A mature person can regulate their own feelings, and they are securely attached to others. Although they are flexible, they can protect their own boundaries. As you encounter the world, stay in tune with your feelings and act on them as needed. If a guy tries to stop you on the street with a hand gesture, you will need to evaluate what it means and if you need to respond. It would be a different response to someone trying to get help from an accident or if it were someone with too much to drink. If a woman comes uncomfortably close or tries to grab your arm in an assertive way, decide whether to move towards or away from her. It could be a helpful soul trying to save you from a moving car, but it may be an unstable or threatening individual trying to hurt you. The response would be different in these scenarios. As you learn to assess, make a choice and examine the outcome, helps you mature.

Set good foundations for the next generation

Parents are the best people to model positive touch to their children. In Chapter 10, we discussed age-appropriate touch interactions to give positive touch and model good behavior in the family.

As your child interacts with her relatives, she can learn how to set her own boundaries of comfortable touch. If she is a highly affectionate child, she can learn how to respect others space before simply jumping on their lap. On the other hand, if she more reserved, her parents can advise family to ask permission for hugs or kisses. Children can be taught what is appropriate and what is allowable touch. He can learn to detect what feels good, bad or confusing on a visceral level. He can learn to share with his parent or a trusted adult if he feels confused or disgusted about someone's interaction. If they develop these skills as younger children, youth will have confidence to remove themselves from awkward or unsafe situations.

Help youth develop what boundaries are considerate of self and others in various situations. Good boundaries are ones that can be adjusted with extra information. For example, people may have personal space bubbles but at a concert, the bubble may be temporarily shrunk to allow for the unintentional body contact as people move around.

Positive affirmations with friends

Surround yourself with people who are receptive to the changes you are making. These people are affectionate and respect their own space and time. Practice with trusted friends to make healthy choices, "That is not good for me, this is what is good for me;" is a helpful phrase to use. Try out new skills in primary relationships with family, friends and your partner and anyone else whose path you cross. Treating yourself well sets the standard for others to follow in how they treat you. Honor and value yourself and others by aiming for good interactions of affirming touch between you.

Learn to ask for time before giving an answer. Some people might internally say no but cower to other people's wishes, while feeling disrespected. Calmly give your answer, expect them to respect you, without offering any explanation.

Remember to be watching and listening for cues from others at the same time. This is not only self-centric but loving towards yourself and others. Ask them questions: What is good for you? What do you like? What do you want? Everyone has differences in the type and quantity of touch they prefer. Being mature is treating yourself and others with honor and care.

Attachment and Adult relationships

The success or failure of your attachments is important. Maintain your internal emotional balance and enjoy the social friction with others. In healthy adult relationships, we can rebound from a disappointment, communicate about conflict and begin anew. Mature adults know how they are feeling and successfully manage stress. They can use body language effectively, are playful in a mutually engaging manner and can relinquish grudges.

Discerning your emotions in response to the actions of others in the moment can help minimize regret. Be aware of how other people respond to you and ask for verbal feedback. For instance, "Hey, I noticed when I tried to touch your hand, you pulled it away. Are you ok? Did I do something to upset you?" Being able to be mature and balanced and helping other people live this way can be rewarding as you live out your new normal.

There seem to be two extremes that individuals without good boundaries can fall into, either ultra-selfish people who deeply care for themselves and no one else, or ultra-giving individuals who forget to tend to themselves. A person who neglects herself might be covertly attempting to make others be off-balanced, to in turn neglect themselves and care for her. She may not have learned the value of good self-care. A person who is self-centered constructs all their relationship on being on the winning side of the arrangement. They appear to have logical ideas as to why they are always on top, but they have not humbled themselves and learned to honor others without expecting a reward.

Finding people who are succeeding in an area, not only possess wisdom but have implemented it in their own lives with success. If a fitness coach, financier, or relationship coach markets a good system but they are a poor example, they are not yet ready to lead. Discern which people follow their own advice, to evaluate if they can be a role model for you. Keep those people close who are in your life who enjoy touch and are emotionally available and have healthy boundaries. Good role models demonstrate what they have learned verbally and with their lives.

Survivors of physical abuse

We cannot always know if someone had mental or physical abuse. Observe a person and let them lead with touch if you see them not wanting to engage with you. It is appropriate to ask to share a hug. If you know they were mistreated, then approach them slowly and gently. Less pressure touch and a shorter-length hug are recommended if they are not used to hugging. If people seem resistant to touch, start a conversation to find out more. Encourage positive touch and respect their boundaries. (domesticshelters, 2018)

A boundary shows me where I end and someone else begins, leading me to a sense of ownership. Knowing what I am to own and take responsibility for gives me freedom. Henry Cloud (Cloud & Townsend, 1992)

Considerate affection demonstrates care about another's well-being in a human, tactile way. It is good and costs nothing to give touch. It is age-irrelevant and always available.

Your new normal includes being aware of the value of touch in your life.

Do I feel good knowing the touch is coming?

Do I feel good during the touch?

Do I feel good after the touch? This is a barometer of the visceral

response you have. How is this touch affecting me?

Is it making me feel better?

Is it making me feel warmer?

Do I feel happier?

Do I get a sick feeling in the pit of my stomach?

Do I want to run away?

Do I want to make it stop?

There is hope for a normal life filled with the loving affection given and received with family and friends. By taking care of yourself spiritually, mentally and physically, you can make steps forward on this path.

If you are parenting children, start early to instill affirming touch as they grow. Friends and professionals can help you sort through your feelings and practice in a safe atmosphere. Approach touch with a curious learning attitude and respectfully interact with others.

Feel Good Now Activity

Keep intact healthy physical and emotional boundaries with others to show respect for their current commitments and relationships.

* * * *

Cloud, H., & Townsend, J. (2017). Boundaries Updated and Expanded Edition: When to Say Yes, How to Say No To Take Control of Your Life (Enlarged ed.). Zondervan.

domesticshelters.org. (2015, August 12). Hugs that Don't Trigger Fear in Survivors. Https://Www.Domesticshelters.Org. https://www.domesticshelters.org/domestic-violence-articles-information/hugs-that-don-t-trigger-fear-in-survivors

Goleman, D. (2005). Emotional Intelligence: Why It Can Matter More Than IQ (10th Anniversary ed.). Bantam

Good Therapy. (2018, May 16). Body Psychotherapy. Https://Www.Goodtherapy.Org/. http://www.goodtherapy.org/body-psychotherapy.html

Hanks, F. (2015). When Your Body Is Not Your Own. Http://Www.Emptyhospitals.Org/. http://www.emptyhospitals.org/when-your-body-is-not-your-own/

Helfer, R. (1984). Childhood Comes First: A Crash Course in Childhood for Adults (2nd ed.). C Henry Kempe.

Hunter, M. G., & Struve, J. (1998). The Ethical Use of Touch in Psychotherapy (And Political Culture). SAGE Publications, Inc.

Mae, S. (2019). The Complicated Heart: Loving Even When It Hurts. B&H Books.

Silverstein, S. (2006). The Missing Piece Meets the Big O (1st ed.). Harper & Row

~~~~

Mariana M. Brosnan

Chapter 16: Where Do We Go From Here?

Christina is a bubbly Chinese-Australian girl in her early twenties. She greets people with a huge embrace and sweet smile. Her group of friends orbit around her touch. By her willingness to be touchy-feely, she has encouraged others to give touch to her and others by her example.

My friend Nate and I arrived late to meet her to go surfing. She tried to physically move away to avoid letting him hug her as he apologized. He knew that if he could say sorry and give her a loving embrace, she would forgive him for being late. Nate used to be more touch-averse but now he warmly hugs both his male and female friends. The Christina-effect has changed her friend-group dynamics. The freely expressed emotions and touch help everyone feel loved and cared for.

One person can affect all the ones around them by developing a culture of touch. Skin hunger has brought to the forefront the slow acceleration of loss of human connection. The absence of personal touch in families and between friends has caused people to suffer in their lives. Mental health conditions such as depression, anxiety and stress are becoming the norm. Loneliness and isolation are leading to unremarkable and shortened lives.

Any past suffering or deprivation must be faced and overcome. There are people to assist you such as trained counselors and psychotherapists. Find someone you can work with and they can clean out the cells' memory of grief and abuse and help you restart. The people around you can also play a role in helping you change as you enlist their help and talk about your experiences and practice your new insights about touch. The world will change in the years ahead and it is up to you to instill more comfort and loving touch into your life and those around you. You can be a catalyst for positive change.

Each person must make their choice to invest the energy to have more pleasant physical interactions. Accessing complementary and alternative medicine such as massage, acupuncture, and chiropractic. can support relational good touch. They can fill in the gap of getting all the great results of lowering pain, regulating blood pressure, toning muscles and improving mood through serotonin boost.

We need the positive eight touches a day to be giving and getting all these positive benefits. The advantage to your health in resisting illness and balancing your vital organs is immense. Emotional regulation and being free from troubles of the past allow a person to successfully navigate their lives forward. Spiritual enhancements from affirmation can include feeling the intimacy with your creator and knowing that you were made for a purpose. Other types of benefits may be getting an increase in salary, tips or wins in sports is a monetary trackable record.

Start today by accessing how great is your personal skin hunger. Do you feel loved and accepted by your family of origin? Do you feel the warmth and care from those around you in your family? Are your friends able to give positive encouragement with touch when you meet for coffee or sports? Do the people at your job seem like they are a team and can offer appropriate congratulatory taps on the shoulder? You can make a difference for yourself and others. You have the tools and it is up to you to implement your knowledge and become someone spreading the Christina-effect.

It is said that every time we embrace someone warmly, we gain an extra day of life. So please embrace me now. (Paulo Coelho, 2011)

Feel Good Now Activity

Next time it rains, put on some celebration

music. Run outside with everyone in your house

and dance in the yard. Dance with everyone,

hold hands and twirl around.

* * * *

Locker, M. (2020, August 4). Alabama Principal Masterfully Turns "U Can't Touch This" Into Everyone's Favorite New Coronavirus Awareness Bop. Time. https://time.com/5875451/u-cant-touch-this/

Paulo Coelho Aleph (First American Edition). (2011). Knopf.

Schwartz, S. (2017, November 7). How a Parent's Affection Shapes a Child's Happiness for Life. Gottman. https://www.gottman.com/blog/how-a-parents-affection-shapes-a-childs-happiness-for-life/

~~~~

Mariana M. Brosnan

Acknowledgments

High 5's to the Cheerleaders who kept asking me when I would finish this book.

Air Kisses to the ones who encouraged me and gave me a quiet place to write:

Michelle & Wolfgang, Malik, Keri & Tim, Rebecca & Juan, Ashley & Judith

Big Hugs to editors Janet and Kim who took some mucky ideas and helped shape them

Fist bump to Photogenius Russ, earlybird Rowrow and creative A and Ms. J.

Love to my family Chevy, Jordano, Kelsey, SGB, Maroyoy, TD, Madre, Jp Pajamas, Pa, and Bevskidoodle

E: Dove sei? Te uncle

Side Hug for those Interviewees

I will keep your name private but this bear hug is for you.

To all the people who tried to crush my dreams, drag me to their level, take my time, energy & resources, used me as a shop, were cruel for your own selfishness, I forgive you. You were a godsend to humble and purify me and by God's grace and to his glory, I am succeeding.

Most of all thank you God for health, good ideas, and never giving up on me.

About the Author

Mariana M. Brosnan grew up in a car between small town Alaska and Costa Rica. She was her family's mediator, looking at motivation and actions of her family. This interest drew her to get a degree in psychology and sociology to find ways to help people live healthier lives.

She believes that everyone can have a more grounded, healed life with more connection to God, yourself and others.

If you have enjoyed this book, please leave a review.
Please enjoy a preview of my next book.

The Two Faces of Love:

Being Unconditionally Loved and Loving Unconditionally

The whole world is screaming out, "LOVE ME!!!, PLEASE, SOMEONE!!??!! ANYONE!!??!! LOVE ME!!! Please???!!." People have decided that perhaps being open-minded to anything that lets someone feel loved is acceptable but this has led to some sort of strange-tolerance to any idea. We know we are missing something because we feel unloved and unaccepted and without purpose. All the things we try, fill us for a while, but after a while, we seek them again and again to fill our empty tank.

In relationship, we go in feeling like we have a half-full cup and looking for someone to fill us up. We end up draining ourselves into someone else hoping they'll return the favor. Gradually we turn outward looking for someone else to fill our cup and know we can only get a measure of satisfaction from that other relationship.

Maybe we give up and look to nurture and fix others pains and hurts. While trying to secretly draw feeling better from our giving actions.

Even teachers or people in authority, who are to invest into others, have tried to take from those who they are entrusted to care for.

How do we fix this madness? How do we fill ourselves up without damaging others? How does God play into any of this? How do we do the steps to get filled up? Is it possible? Was that the intention in life anyway? Or is achieving whatever dream you thought or become what you can be the thing we must settle for? Is it for some sort of deeply dissatisfying life?

Mariana M. Brosnan

I believe we were created for more and it is achievable and we should go after the best. I also believe it is easier and harder than we all think.

A new book coming June 2021 from author Mariana M. Brosnan Discover other titles coming soon at
www.MarianaMBrosnan.com

~~~~

My sweet friends,

Let this life not end with us apart and wishing we would have embraced one more time.

M.

~~~~

Made in the USA
Middletown, DE
24 April 2022